1

NORMAL SCHOOL EDUCATION AND EFFICIENCY IN TEACHING

AMS PRESS
NEW YORK

COLUMBIA UNIVERSITY, TEACHERS COLLEGE

CONTRIBUTIONS TO EDUCATION

NO. 1

NORMAL SCHOOL EDUCATION AND EFFICIENCY IN TEACHING

BY

JUNIUS LATHROP MERIAM, Ph. D.

Adjunct Professor of Education, University of Missouri

PUBLISHED BY

Teachers College, Columbia University

NEW YORK

1906

Library of Congress Cataloging in Publication Data
Meriam, Junius Lathrop, 1872-
    Normal school education and efficiency in teaching.
    Original ed. issued as no. 1 of Columbia University,
Teachers College. Contributions to education.
    Originally presented as the author's thesis, Columbia.
    Bibliography: p.
    1. Teachers colleges — United States. 2. Teachers,
Training of — United States. 3. Educational psychology.
I. Title. II. Series: Columbia University. Teachers
College. Contributions to education, no. 1.
LB1715.M39 1972   370'.73   77 - 177071
ISBN 0-404-55001-0
ISBN 0-404-55000-2 (SET)

Reprinted by Special Arrangement with Teachers
College Press, Columbia University, New York

From the edition of 1906: New York
First AMS edition published in 1972
Manufactured in the United States

AMS PRESS, INC.
NEW YORK, N.Y. 10003

CONTENTS

CHAPTER I

CHAPTER II

PSYCHOLOGY IN THE CURRICULUM FOR TEACHERS

CHAPTER III

OPINIONS OF STUDENTS AS TO THE VALUE OF NORMAL SCHOOL PSYCHOLOGY

CHAPTER VI

THE INSTRUCTORS IN THE NEW YORK STATE NORMAL SCHOOLS

NORMAL SCHOOL EDUCATION AND EFFICIENCY IN TEACHING

CHAPTER I

INTRODUCTION

THE five studies here collected relate to the work of Normal Schools as training institutions, and to the efficiency of teachers in the elementary schools. They all bear upon the problem of the relation between ability to teach and proficiency in previous study and training.

There is room for much more emphasis upon limiting the work of the Normal Schools to the preparation of teachers for elementary schools, instead of attempting, as some do, to prepare superintendents and principals in town high schools, as well as special teachers in high schools. This is particularly true where such teachers, principals and superintendents have had no more advanced education than that offered in our secondary schools. On the letter-heads used by one of these Normal School graduates a statement is made of the various courses of study and of the opportunities offered in his school, after which are the words: " College preparatory work our specialty." Here is an illustration of how the Normal Schools tend to place their graduates in secondary school positions, and how these teachers undertake work which cannot be efficiently done with' so limited training.

Such tendencies carry with them the implication that the

elementary school does not present the real educational problems found in the higher work. An educational institution is doing real work when it is delving into vital educational problems. If the elementary field did not offer such problems, to enter the higher fields is of course advisable. The present studies may serve, however, to point out some problems of the lower grades that need study. That scarcely any of such work is now done in the Normal Schools may find some explanation in one of the present studies, that on the instructors in the State Normal Schools of New York.

The first study given here is of an historical nature, inquiring briefly into the beginning and rise of the study of psychology in Normal Schools (confined here to the United States). It will be seen that the study of psychology has been a prominent factor in the curriculum from the first, but that the nature of this work has been very general and even indefinite, and that its improvement has not kept pace with the advances of psychology itself.

The second study is that of a questionnaire on the contribution made by Normal School psychology to efficiency in teaching. This is based wholly on the personal opinion of Normal School graduates now teaching, hence generalizations can be made only provisionally. The evidence, direct and indirect, shows that the work of the schools in psychology is vague, loose, and in need of reconstruction.

The third is a statistical study of the relations between teaching efficiency and scholarship in the various studies pursued by teachers in their Normal School course. This involves a study of 1,185 teachers, and about 25,000 individual records of scholarship. Here success in practice-teaching and in the study of psychology are found to be the largest contributors to efficiency in teaching. The study also suggests that the emphasis given to "Methods" is ill-placed; that subject-matter courses themselves take slightly higher rank than such " Methods." Further, the study shows weakness in present methods of grading scholarship in school work. Another method is suggested.

The fourth study deals very briefly with the general preparation of elementary teachers. After a year or so, experience seems to contribute little, if any, to efficiency. That is, teachers with two years' experience have as high a rank as those with five, ten, or fifteen years' experience. More or less than a four-years' high school course makes no difference. College graduates are less successful in the lower grades. Professional work in Normal Schools does not contribute as much as one would expect, though Normal School graduates do better than teachers trained in city training schools, and these in turn better than teachers with no pedagogical education at all.

The fifth study inquires concerning the qualifications of the teachers in the State Normal Schools of New York. Only about one-fourth of these are college graduates, and one-third have never studied further than the Normal Schools in which they are teaching. This characteristic of the teaching staffs is supported further by a detailed study of one of the schools throughout its history; also, by a study of forty-nine representative Normal Schools throughout the country, outside of New York; and lastly, by the slight contributions made to current pedagogical literature by Normal School teachers.

The outline in the presentation of these studies is:
  1. Introduction, stating—
     (1) The problem.
     (2) The general conclusions.
  2. Method of treating the study.
  3. Details of the study.
  4. Generalizations and conclusions, more in detail.

CHAPTER II

PSYCHOLOGY IN THE CURRICULUM FOR TEACHERS

INTRODUCTION

1. The Problem.

What has decided the nature of the professional training of teachers? The introduction and development of psychology is taken as a type for study.

The subjects of study pursued by those preparing for the work of a teacher are, in the main, selected according to the personal opinion of those in charge, or are now used because of their traditional standing. No pedagogical curriculum has ever been worked out by scientific method; no scientific tests have ever been applied to the usual subjects in the curriculum to see what relative value they have in the preparation of the teacher. We have, therefore, only traditional standing and personal opinion to guide us. To point out what this opinion is (with reference to one subject, psychology) and to show how opinion has developed in the preparation of the teacher in the elementary schools is the purpose of this chapter.

2. Generalizations Reached.

The points of emphasis in this chapter may be seen in the following brief outline:

   1. The present requirements in the preparation of the teacher, with special reference to psychology.

      1. Examinations for state certificates ask for some knowledge of psychology in a majority of cases.

    2. Certificates to teach, given by colleges and universities, make this same requirement, with but few exceptions.

    3. Diplomas from State Normal Schools invariably require psychology.

2. The development of the idea that psychology is needed in courses for teachers.

    1. Though the Normal School idea was first presented in 1789, it was not until 1825 that open opinion was expressed in favor of the study of mind as essential for teachers. This contained no clear idea of the scope or content of psychology, but was a demand for the study of mental phenomena, so far as possible at that time.

    2. Study in the philosophy of mind was present in all the early Normal Schools, due to the conception that the science of education and the art of teaching were based on the philosophy of mind, but the great need of academic work in the common branches made this subject secondary.

    3. Its development from 1839 until recent years was very slow, and its content was very indefinite. Its character seems closely allied to moral philosophy.

    4. Its more rapid development in some schools since about 1897 seems to be due, in part, to influence from the National Educational Association.

This chapter assumes:

1. That the Normal School is, at present, the leading institution in the training of elementary teachers, and that the development of the idea that psychology is essential in the courses is representative of that of other subjects.

2. That the belief in the value of psychology—whatever be the truth or error in the idea—is based, not upon knowledge and measurement, but upon personal opinion and custom.

3. That a better criterion for the worth of any subject in the curriculum for teachers is found in a statistical study; and that in this study an approximation is made to a knowledge of the quantitative worth of any subject in such courses.

Present Requirements in Psychology for the Preparation of Teachers

It may be safely said that teachers qualify for their positions in one or more of three ways:

1. Certificates secured through state, county or local examination.

2. Certificates granted for work done in schools of education, as in colleges and universities.

3. Diplomas given in recognition of courses pursued in Normal Schools (here including City Training Schools).

The character of the work required as presented by these three methods indicates what is commonly regarded as essential in the equipment of a teacher.

I. STATE EXAMINATIONS

The state of New York issues three grades of certificates to teach. The lowest, or third grade, is a license to teach for one year. Examinations must be passed in the following subjects: American History, Arithmetic, Grammar, English Composition, Geography, Orthography, Penmanship, Physiology and Hygiene, School Law, and Reading. The second grade certificate is a license for three years, granted upon the completion of ten weeks of experience in teaching and of examinations in the following subjects in addition to those for the third grade: Civil Government, Current Topics, Drawing, Methods and School Management. The first grade certificate is a license for ten years, given upon the completion of two years of teaching experience and the passing of examinations, in addition to those in the two grades above, in Algebra, Bookkeeping, History of Education, and Physics.[1]

Chapter 329 of the Acts of 1894 of the Massachusetts Legislature, approved April 28, 1894, directs that "the Board of Education shall cause to be held public examinations of candidates for the positions of teachers in the public schools of the Commonwealth. Such examinations shall test the professional as well as the scholastic abilities of the candidates." The Secretary of the Board states that the law has not been carried into effect, because of insufficient appropriation. "This [permission to teach without examination] is in sympathy with the general Massachusetts spirit in things educational, a spirit that invites and tries to convince before it positively commands."[2] "The Massachusetts ideal is a system of state licensing whose standards shall be above those of the Normal schools and colleges. . . . The system implies, for the present, a voluntary basis, since its standards are higher than could be maintained on a compulsory basis. It does not require the teacher to hold a state license or the school committee to demand it."[3]

Ohio grants two state certificates good for life:

1. Common schools: Examinations are given in Orthography, Reading, Writing, Arithmetic, Algebra, Geography, English Grammar and Composition, History of the United

---

[1] Report of State Superintendent of New York for 1902, pp. 167-169.

[2] Report of Massachusetts State Board of Education, 1899-1900, p. 228.

[3] *Ibid.*, 1899-1900, p. 230.

States including Civil Government, General History, English Literature, Physiology and Hygiene, Physics, Theory and Practice of Teaching, and Scientific Temperance.

2. High schools: In addition to the above, examinations in Geometry, Rhetoric, Civil Government, Latin, Psychology, History of Education, Science of Education. Also three branches from the following: Chemistry, Botany, Zoölogy, Geology, Astronomy, Trigonometry, Logic, Greek, German, Political Economy.[1]

Illinois [2] grants two state certificates; one for five years, the other for life. The former calls for examinations in the usual academic work; the latter increases the academic work, and adds " Pedagogy."

Two state certificates are granted in Iowa,[3] High School and Elementary. Under the former "Graduates of the college of liberal arts of the state university, who have pursued in addition to the course in psychology, a pedagogical course of at least one year . . . will be admitted to the examinations. . . . School Management, Elementary Psychology, and Methods of Instruction constitute the examination in this subject " (Didactics). An examination in the " Psychology of the Child " is required of elementary teachers.

In Missouri, " all applicants for state certificates will be examined in . . . psychology." [4] The state report for 1904 makes psychology optional.

In New Hampshire, " permanent certificates " require examinations in psychology and the history of education.

In Michigan and Colorado, I find no mention of psychology in examinations.

[1] Report, Commissioner of Common Schools, 1902, p. 19.
[2] Report, Illinois Board of Education, 1900-1902, p. 29.
[3] Report, Iowa Board of Education, 1902-1903, p. 140-142.
[4] Report, Missouri State Superintendent of Schools, 1897, p. 24.

These nine states may be taken as representative states, or better, as leading states. The importance of such data in this particular investigation does not call for a larger representation of states.

Examinations for state certificates only have been considered. It is well known that county, township, and local examinations vary much, but the probability is that such examinations are considerably directed by those for the state certificates.

2. COLLEGES AND UNIVERSITIES

Consider, secondly, requirements in the various schools of education in colleges and universities.

Teachers College of Columbia University offers a four years' course leading to the degree of Bachelor of Science in Education. The first two years' work is considered collegiate, though arranged with a view to later professional work.

Students in the Collegiate Course are required to take work during the freshman and sophomore years amounting to a total of thirty points. The courses necessary to meet these requirements may be chosen by the student at will—from those designated in the annual Announcement by letters and by the numbers 1-9 inclusive—subject to the approval of the Committee on Undergraduate Students, and according to the general regulations of the College and the following:

OUTLINE OF COURSE

(A) For all students:

1—ENGLISH A—Rhetoric and Composition—3 points.

2—ENGLISH 2 or 5—Literature—2 points.

3—BIOLOGY AND PHYSICAL EDUCATION 3 } Physiology and Hygiene } 2 points.

4—And courses amounting to 2 points in FINE ARTS, MUSIC, or MANUAL TRAINING.

(B) Students who do not offer the following subjects at entrance must take in college the courses appearing opposite them (unless a more advanced course in the same department be elected), namely,

Entrance Subjects.	*College Courses.*
1—German	German A—3 points.
2—French	French A—3 points or German 2—3 points.
3—Advanced Mathematics	Mathematics A or B—3 points.
4—Advanced History	History A—3 points.

(C) Also two of the courses following, unless the subjects appearing in connection with them are offered at entrance:

1—Chemistry	Physical Science 1—2 points.
2—Physics	Physical Science 2—2 points.
3—Botany	Biology 1—2 points.
4—Zoölogy	Biology 2—2 points.
5—Physiography	Geography 1—2 points.

(D) All students in the freshman and sophomore years of the Collegiate Course are required to take systematic physical exercise two hours weekly, under the direction of the Professor of Physical Education. Students may meet this requirement by taking, with credit, Physical Education 1 or 2.

Electives should be selected with a view to the Professional Course that is to follow.

Courses in Education (except Psychology A and Education 10, which are recommended to qualified sophomores) are not open to collegiate students.[1]

The last two years are considered professional. If taken without the two years of collegiate work, they lead to Bachelors' diplomas. The following is the course leading to the diploma in elementary education:

JUNIOR YEAR

Prescribed (5 points): PSYCHOLOGY A—Elements of psychology, *and* EDUCATION 10—Educational psychology—(together) 3 points.

EDUCATION 12—Child study—2 points.

[1] Teachers College Announcement, 1904-1905, pp. 35-37.

Elective (10-13 points): (*a*) Recommended for primary teachers:

 Biology and Physical Education 3, Education 16, English A, English 2 or 5, English 10, Geography 1, History A, Manual Training 1 and 27, Mathematics B, Music 1, Nature Study 10 and 12.

 (*b*) Recommended for grammar grade teachers:

 Biology 1, Biology 2, Biology and Physical Education 3, English A, English 2 or 5, Geography 1 or 2, History A, History 2, Mathematics B, Manual Training 1 and 27, Music 1, Physical Science 1, Physical Science 2.

SENIOR YEAR

Prescribed (8 points): EDUCATION 50—History and principles of education—3 points.

 EDUCATION 15—General method and practice teaching—3 points.

 EDUCATION 20, 26, 32, 38, or 46, with practical work—2 points.

Elective (7-10 points): (*a*) Recommended for primary teachers:

 Education 20—Nature Study; Education 26—English; Education 32—Geography; Education 46—Mathematics; Fine Arts 3, Geography 1 or 2, Music 2.

 (*b*) Recommended for grammar grade teachers:

 Education 20—Nature Study; Education 26—English; Education 32—Geography; Education 38—History; Education 46—Mathematics; Domestic Art 12, Fine Arts 3, Geography 1, 2, or 3, History 10, Music 2.[1]

Similar courses are outlined for teachers in secondary schools, teachers of kindergarten, domestic art, domestic science, fine arts, manual training, music, physical education. These subjects are common to all as prescribed work: Elements of psychology, educational psychology, and history and principles of education. All graduate

[1] Teachers College Announcement, 1904-1905, pp. 39-40.

diplomas or degrees require of the candidate educational psychology, and history and principles of education, as well as ability to read French and German.

The College of Education in Chicago University outlines the following two years' course for teachers in the elementary schools: [1]

Philosophy and Education	3	points.
History, English, and Oral Reading	3	"
Arts	2	"
Mathematics	1	"
Science	3	"
Electives	6	"
(Total required)	18	"

Specific prerequisites for this work are Psychology, Ethics, and Educational Theory—two points. For secondary and Normal School teachers, " Psychology and Ethics are required as antecedents." In General Course A four points in psychology are required.

The Teachers College of the University of Missouri, which began its work in the fall of 1904, offers a four years' course leading to the degree of Bachelor of Science in Education. One hundred and twenty (120) hours of work are required. (This means 15 hours of class attendance each week.) Further requirements of the student are: " He must complete work in education to the amount of 24 hours, including Practice Teaching (3 to 9 hours credit) and Educational Psychology." " He must complete a course in General Psychology with at least 3 hours credit. This course must be completed before the Junior year. Additional work in Psychology, or work in Ethics or in Sociology, may be required by the instructor in charge of any course in education." [2]

---

[1] Chicago University Annual Register, 1902-1903, pp. 137-138.

[2] Catalogue, University of Missouri, 1904-1905, pp. 143-144.

Life certificates to teach in the secondary and elementary schools require the same amount of education and psychology. To secure a two years' certificate, the candidate must take education and psychology to the extent of at least half that required for the degree.

In the specifications of the Department of Education of the University of California, the following statement is made: " The undergraduate courses are reserved for the third and fourth years of college residence. Students who purpose taking any of the courses in education are advised to prepare for the study by taking one or more of the courses in psychology. After the year 1903-4, Philosophy 2 (general psychology) will be made a prerequisite of all undergraduate courses in the department." [1]

In the University of Wisconsin, psychology is required for teachers' certificates, granted by the university under the regulation of the state.[2]

Cornell University requires, for the New York State college-graduate certificate, history of education and principles of education or psychological basis of education.[3]

In Dartmouth College, psychology is " strongly recommended as a preparation for the courses in education." [4]

The University of Cincinnati requires psychology in its Teachers' College.[5]

In the University of Michigan,[6] three courses are required for both the teachers' diploma and the teachers' certificate: Practical Pedagogy (text, Gordy's *A Broader Ele-*

---

[1] Catalogue, University of California, 1904, p. 136.

[2] Catalogue, University of Wisconsin, 1903-1904, p. 94.

[3] Cornell Register, 1904-1905, pp. 131-132.

[4] Catalogue, Dartmouth College, 1903-1904, p. 147.

[5] Catalogue, 1903-1904, p. 178.

[6] Catalogue of the University of Michigan, 1903-1904, pp. 92, 93, 124.

mentary Education); The Art of Study (text, Hinsdale's *The Art of Study*); Theoretical and Critical Pedagogy (text, Harris' *Psychological Foundations of Education*).

These nine colleges and universities represent adequately the leading ones giving work in education.

3. NORMAL SCHOOLS

The first Normal School in this country was founded at Lexington, in 1839. Within that year three more were started in Massachusetts. New York followed with one at Albany, in 1844. Other schools were established rapidly until in Massachusetts there are now eight; in New York, twelve; in the whole country, one hundred and eleven.

The schools referred to here are State Public Normal Schools. The United States Commissioner's Report for 1902 gives the following classification of all Normal Schools: [1]

1. Public Normal Schools..............................173
2. Private Normal Schools............................109
3. Public Normal Schools in universities and colleges... 39
4. Private Normal Schools in universities and colleges.. 195
5. Public Normal Schools in high schools.............. 368
6. Private Normal Schools in high schools.............. 357

The type of the third and fourth classes has already been indicated in the treatment of schools of education in colleges and universities. The fifth and sixth classes are probably intended to include many of the city training classes, the work of which is similar to that of the regular Normal Schools, though usually more limited in character and scope.

The curricula in the various State Normal Schools in any

[1] Report, Commissioner of Education, 1902, p. 1581.

given state are quite uniform, being usually prepared by state officials, or by the joint action of the principals of the various schools. In most schools the work is wholly prescribed.

The general course of study prescribed by the Board of Education of Massachusetts for the schools of that state is the following:

1. Psychology, history of education, principles of teaching, methods of instruction and discipline, school organization, school laws of Massachusetts.

2. Methods of teaching the following subjects:

(*a*) English—reading, language, composition, literature, history.

(*b*) Mathematics—arithmetic, bookkeeping, elementary algebra, and geometry.

(*c*) Science—elementary physics and chemistry, geography, physiology and hygiene, study of minerals, plants, and animals.

(*d*) Drawing, vocal music, physical training, manual training.

3. Observation and practice in the training school, and observation in other public schools.[1]

This course of study was adopted May 6, 1880. Provision is made for four other courses, mere modifications of this one, which is planned as a two years' course for those intending to teach in the elementary schools of the state. The equivalent of a high school education is required for admission. The time devoted to each subject varies in the different schools.

The schools of New York state have four courses, which were adopted September 1, 1900.[2] Two of these courses are for those students who are not graduates of high schools. These are four years in length. The other two are for high school graduates, and are two years in length, as follows:

[1] Westfield (Mass.) Catalogue for 1901.
[2] New Paltz (N. Y.) Year Book, 1902-1903.

Classical and English

Those in the English course omit the ancient and modern language requirements below and substitute 5 hours of work per week under advice of division adviser. Classical students omit economics and astronomy.

FIRST YEAR

First Semester	*Second Semester*
Rhetoric 4	English literature 4
Psychology 4	Psychology and General meth. 4
Math. review 1st 10 wk. 4	Science meth. 2d 10 wk. 4
Prim. meth. 1st 10 wk. 4	Arithmetic meth. 4
Geog. meth. 4	Music 1st 10 wk. 2
Drawing 2d 10 wk. 4	Music meth. 3d 5 wk. 4
Grammar meth. 4	Geog. meth. 1st 10 wk. 4
Music 2d 10 wk. 2	Lang. meth. 1st 10 wk. 4
	Draw. meth. 4th 5 wk. 4

SECOND YEAR

First Semester	*Second Semester*
Latin review 5	Civics 2d 10 wk.
Adv. U. S. hist. 5	Greek, French or German IV
Num. meth. 2d 10 wk. 4	Hist. of ed. 1st 10 wk. 5
Economics or Library economy 3	Astronomy 1st wk. 3
Grammar meth. 4	School law 2d 10 wk. 5
School Econ. 1st 10 wk. 5	Teaching
Teaching	

Child Study once a week during the year.[1]

The time given to each subject is not uniform in the various schools. Other slight modifications are made to meet local conditions. The last catalogue of the State Normal College [2] at Albany shows quite an innovation in the curricula offered. Many elective courses are opened, but certain subjects are required, such as Psychology, History of Education, Philosophy of Education, etc.

The State Normal Schools of Wisconsin have the following course designated by the Board of Regents: [3]

[1] New Paltz (N. Y.) Year Book, 1902-1903.

[2] Circular and Announcement, 1904, pp. 12-21.

[3] Catalogue, Oshkosh Normal School, 1901, p. 63.

JUNIOR YEAR

First Quarter
Observation
German, or other language
Drawing
Rhetoric

Third Quarter
Theory
German
Drawing
Music
Physics

Second Quarter
Theory
German
Drawing
School Law (½)
Professional Reading (½)

Fourth Quarter
School Management
Professional Geography
German
Algebra
Music

SENIOR YEAR

First Quarter
Practice Teaching
Professional Arithmetic
Psychology
Geometry

Third Quarter
History of Education
Professional English
Elective Science
Literature

Second Quarter
Economics
Professional History (½)
Professional Gymnastics (½)
Psychology
Practice Teaching

Fourth Quarter
Science of Education
Practice Teaching
Elective Science
Literature

The Normal Schools of California are well represented by the one at Los Angeles. Its course of study is:[1]

FIRST YEAR

	Middle B	*Middle A*
Professional		
English	Psychology 20–4	Psychology 20–4
	Composition, etc., 20–4	
Science	Physiology 20–4	Biology 20–4
	Domestic Science 20–2	Domestic Science 20–3
Geography and History		U. S. History 20–4
Art and Manual Training	Drawing 20–2	Drawing 20–3
	Sloyd 20–2	Sloyd 20–3
Miscellaneous	Reading 20–4	
	Music 20–2	Music 20–2
	Physical Culture 20–2	Physical Culture 20–3

[1] Catalogue, Los Angeles Normal School, 1901.

SECOND YEAR

	Senior B	Senior A
Professional	Hist. & Phil. of Ed. 20-3	School Law 20-2
	General Pedagogy 20-3	School Economy 10-3
		Teaching 20-12½
English	Pedagogy of Grammar 20-3	Lit. in the grades 20-2
		Method in Language 20-1
Science	Pedagogy of Physics 20-2	Method in Biology 20-1
Geography and History	Pedagogy of Geography 20-4	Method in History 20-1
		Method in Geography 20-1
Mathematics	Pedagogy of Arith. 20-5	Method in Arith. 20-1
Art and Manual Training	Pedagogy of Drawing 20-2	Method in Drawing 20-1
Miscellaneous	Pedagogy of Music 20-1	Method in Reading 20-1
		Method in Music 20-1
	Pedagogy of Phy. Cult. 20-2	Method in Phy. Cult. 20-2

The schools of these four states represent adequately the leading Normal Schools of the country.

In these three groups of institutions, aiming to prepare teachers for their work, the emphasis upon psychology as an essential is evident.

1. Examinations (leading to state certificates).

    Nine leading states are here represented.

    Four distinctly require psychology.

    One requires " professional " work.

    One requires "pedagogy" (whatever this includes).

    Three call for academic work only.

2. Universities (granting teachers' certificates).

    Nine leading institutions are represented here.

    Seven distinctly require psychology.

    One strongly recommends psychology.

    One makes no mention of psychology, as such.

3. Normal Schools (granting diplomas and certificates).

    Four states, including about 30 of the leading schools, are here represented.

    All distinctly require work in psychology. (So far as I could ascertain, in looking over about 100 catalogues of State Normal Schools, psychology is included in all.)

Development of the Idea that Psychology is Essential in the Training of Teachers

I. Before Normal Schools Took Up This Work

Gordy has written on the *Rise and Growth of the Normal School Idea* in the United States.[1] He says that the first suggestion of this which he finds is in the Massachusetts Magazine for June, 1789. Here it is stated: " There should be a public grammar school established in each county in the state in which should be taught English Grammar, Latin, Greek, Rhetoric, Geography, Mathematics, etc., in order to fit young gentlemen for college and school teaching." The famous school law of 1647 gave to the towns of Massachusetts a grammar school. The grammar school here referred to is, therefore, more especially intended for the training of teachers. Gordy speaks further of the contribution to the Normal School idea given by Olmsted, of Yale, 1816; by Kingsley, of Yale, in 1823; also by Russel, of the New Haven Academy, and editor of the *American Journal of Education*, in 1823; and by Hall, who is recognized as the first principal of the first teachers' seminary in America, at Concord, in 1823. Here was prepared his *Lectures on School Keeping*, a brief outline of which is given in Barnard's *American Journal of Education*, vol. 5, p. 388.

While the contributors mentioned emphasize the need of training schools for teachers, none of them gives expression to the need of studying other subjects than those which are to be taught.

In 1825, in the Boston *Patriot*, published by James G. Carter, appeared a series of articles with the signature

[1] Also found in the United States Bureau of Education, Circulars of Information, 1891, No. 8, pp. 1-142.

" Franklin," giving suggestions for an institution for the training of teachers.[1] It was there maintained that such an institution should " open up a new science somewhat peculiar to itself in the science of the development of the human mind. . . . The philosophy of the infant mind must be understood by the instructor before much progress can be made in the science of education. . . . Every book, therefore, which would aid in an analysis of the youthful mind should be placed in the library of the proposed institution." This is the first expression I find on the need of studying mental phenomena in the preparation of a teacher. Various other articles appear about this time in the Boston *Patriot, North American Review, United States Review, Literary Gazette,* but these advocate the founding of teachers' seminaries without going into detail. In the same year, 1825, Johnson issued a pamphlet on " The Need of Attending Lectures on the Science of Mental Development." [2]

In 1830 a school for the training of teachers was attached to Phillips Academy, at Andover. S. R. Hall was made principal. The course of study contains " intellectual philosophy " in the third year.[3]

In 1830, J. G. Carter, Secretary of the Massachusetts Board of Education, and often called the " Father of American Normal Schools," wrote an article on " Development of Intellectual Faculties." [4] Here he speaks strongly in favor of the study of mind as a requisite in the preparation of a teacher. " The foundations of a teacher's pro-

---

[1] Portions are quoted in Barnard, *On Normal Schools,* p. 75 *et seq.*

[2] Gordy, *supra,* p. 14.

[3] Barnard, *American Journal of Education,* vol. v, p. 379.

[4] *American Institute of Instruction,* 1830, pp. 52-95.

fessional skill are laid in an intimate acquaintance with the conditions, states, and wants of the youthful mind." He attempts a practical application in a lesson on map-drawing, the methods of which are much like the methods of to-day.

A. R. Baker, in the same periodical three years later, repeats the thought in an article " On the Adaptation of Intellectual Philosophy to Instruction." [1] His emphasis is upon the intimate relation between intellectual philosophy and education. Intellectual philosophy is defined as " a science of the human mind which investigates its phenomena, and applies the results of the investigation to the practical purposes of active life."

In 1833, Dr. Channing speaks of the importance of having the teacher comprehend " the mind in all its capacities, tracing out the laws of thought and moral actions, understanding the perfection of human nature." [2]

J. Gregg, in 1835, is yet more emphatic in writing on " The Importance of an Acquaintance with the Philosophy of Mind to an Instructor." [3] He says this is not mere psychology. " It does not consist merely in the observation and arbitrary classification of the phenomena of the conscious states of the mind." It is rather " the knowledge of man as an intellectual and spiritual being—of his natures, powers, capacities, habitudes, wants—of the laws and principles that regulate the various mental and moral phenomena which he exhibits." The article aims to show that the philosophy of mind teaches the true (1) nature, (2) method, (3) means, and (4) ends of education. It is here very clear, as the article claims, that by the philosophy of mind

---

[1] *American Institute of Instruction*, 1833, pp. 263-288.

[2] Quoted by Barnard, *On Normal Schools*, p. 93.

[3] *American Institute of Instruction*, 1835, pp. 111-131.

is intended what was then known as a scientific study of psychology, and also a philosophy of education.

By act of the Legislature of New York, May 2, 1834, the Regents of the University were authorized to apply a part of the income of the Literature Fund to educate the teachers of the common schools. In the following year, 1835,[1] a plan was put into effect whereby a department for the training of teachers was grafted upon selected academies.

The course of study for teachers included the following:
1. The English Language.
2. Writing and Drawing.
3. Arithmetic, Mental and Written, and Bookkeeping.
4. The History of the United States.
5. Geometry, Trigonometry, Mensuration, and Surveying.
6. Geography and General History (continued).
7. Natural Philosophy and the Elements of Astronomy.
8. Chemistry and Mineralogy.
9. The Constitution of the United States and of New York.
10. Select Parts of the Revised Statutes and the Duties of Public Officers.
11. Moral and Intellectual Philosophy.
12. The Principles of Teaching.[2]

This indicates that the academies perceived the need of giving to teachers a different kind of curriculum from the mere academic work. Yet this intellectual philosophy is probably not specially for teachers, as it is found in An-

---

[1] *First Quarto—Centennial History*—Potsdam Normal School, p. 17.
[2] Report, State Superintendent, 1836-1837, pp. 41-42.

dover Academy in 1848, and in Albany Academy in 1874,[1] when this work had passed from the academy to the Normal School. But in the rise of Normal Schools, the academies lost the work of training teachers. Horace Mann, in 1839, in advocating Normal Schools for Massachusetts, opposed the academies of New York on the ground that in these the teachers' training department was only grafted on, while for real success it should be the principal part; hence the need of a distinct institution, the Normal School.

These few expressions are types of many other opinions of those early years as to one particular subject of study needed by those who would be teachers. No reader will find in any of these writings a detailed conception of psychology, nor of what it has to offer to the prospective teacher. Yet one cannot fail to feel the insistence made that the study of mind is essential in preparing for efficient teaching. The public advocacy of such beliefs was a forerunner of what was soon to be found in Normal Schools.

2. IN THE NORMAL SCHOOLS

1. Early Normal Schools.

The first course of study for Normal Schools was adopted by the Board of Education of Massachusetts in 1840. It was as follows, and is essentially that outlined by Horace Mann the year before at the opening of the work at Lexington:

1. Orthography, Reading, Grammar, Composition and Rhetoric, Logic.
2. Writing, Drawing.
3. Arithmetic, Mental and Written; Algebra; Geometry; Bookkeeping; Navigation; Surveying.
4. Geography, Ancient and Modern, with Chronology, Statistics, and General History.

[1] See Catalogue for these years.

5. Physiology.
6. Mental Philosophy.
7. Music.
8. Constitution and History of Massachusetts and the United States.
9. Natural Philosophy, and Astronomy.
10. Natural History.
11. The Principles of Piety and Morality, common to all sects of Christians.
12. *The Science and Art of Teaching, with reference to all the above-named studies.*[1] [The italics show the emphasis intended at that time.]

In his opposition to the attempt of the House of Representatives in Massachusetts, in 1840, to break up the Normal Schools, Mr. Geo. B. Emerson, formerly principal of the Boston High School, based his arguments upon three prominent features of the work as carried on by Cyrus Pierce, principal of the Normal School at Lexington. The second of these features was the emphasis upon leading prospective teachers to an acquaintance with the minds and character of children.[2]

Dr. Samuel Howe, director of the Institute for the Blind in Boston, reported his observations of the work at Lexington. " To me, sir, it was delightful to see how they [the students] were becoming acquainted with the nature of the children's minds BEFORE they undertook to manage them. . . . Every one was desirous of becoming acquainted with the philosophy of mind." [3]

[1] *Common School Journal*, 1839, pp. 37-38. See also Barnard, *On Normal Schools*, pp. 56-57.

[2] *Common School Journal*, 1840, p. 237.

[3] *Common School Journal*, 1840, p. 238.

The attempt 'of the House of Representatives failed, and the Normal Schools, under the lead of Horace Mann, continued and maintained " mental science," or " philosophy of the mind " (various names were used), as one of the requisites in the training of teachers.

The first Normal School of New York state was founded at Albany in 1844. Its first course of study included Abercrombie's *Intellectual Philosophy*.[1]

The first Normal school in Connecticut was founded at New Britain in 1850. The catalogue shows as a portion of the course " The Art of Teaching and its Methods, including the history and progress of education, the philosophy of teaching and discipline, as drawn from the nature of the juvenile mind. . . ."[2]

These few schools referred to are doubtless typical of all early Normal Schools. The following generalizations are easily made, in studying further the courses of study offered:

1. The Normal Schools had a conception that the science of education and the art of teaching were in some way based on the philosophy of mind, but,

2. The need of a more thorough knowledge of the academic work was so great that the instruction in the common branches was the chief work of these schools, so that,

3. Work in intellectual philosophy was rather secondary, and that, too, quite vague. But in the work of these early schools there is a distinct beginning of the teaching of psychology as essential in the preparation of the teacher.

2. *Sixty Years of Normal School Work.*

An examination of the catalogues of the Normal Schools of Massachusetts and New York from their beginning to

---

[1] Register and Circular, 1846, p. 16.

[2] Barnard, *On Normal Schools*, pp. 48-49.

the present time; as also the State Annual Reports of these schools (which are very meager) lead one to the following conclusions:

1. Mental philosophy of some kind—even if only in name—has been in the courses of study from the beginning.

2. This subject has always been very vague and indefinite; yet it evidenced a constant endeavor to point to an important relation between the ability to teach and the knowledge of mental activity.

3. This subject is mixed up with other educational subjects, such as the history of education, philosophy of education, general method, etc. It has usually been taught by the principal of the school in connection with the other subjects mentioned. (At present, there are only three schools in Massachusetts which have special teachers of psychology, and in New York only five.)

4. There is no distinct time when "Psychology," as such, first appeared. It is thus mentioned first in Westfield, 1867; Bridgewater, 1869; Framingham, 1876. But there is no indication that the name changed the character of the work.

5. There is no indication of any uniformity in the character of the work done, though the aims of the work, as stated in the catalogues of the various schools, are in close agreement. The only effort towards united action in this respect is that which was taken by the Wisconsin Normal Schools in an institute held at Oshkosh, December 17–21, 1900, when the schools of the state agreed upon and formulated aims, content, and method of the work to be done in psychology.

6. There is striking evidence of a great lack of development in this work from the beginning. However, in a few schools, quite a change has been made in recent years, particularly since 1897. This recent change seems due largely

to the pressure brought to bear by the Normal School department of the National Educational Association. The work of this organization in this particular can be summed up briefly.

3. The Influence of the National Educational Association.

The National Educational Association began in 1858, as the National Teachers' Association. The Normal School department gave the subject of psychology no attention until 1863. For the next decade various well-known men gave addresses emphasizing the value of psychology in the preparation of the teacher (in 1863, Dr. Sheldon,[1] of the Oswego Normal School; in 1864, President Hill,[2] of Harvard; in 1865, President Edwards,[3] of the Illinois Normal University; in 1866, W. F. Phelps,[4] of the Winona (Wis.) Normal School; in 1871, J. W. Dickinson,[5] principal of the Westfield (Mass.) Normal School). Whatever general influence these addresses may have had, no definite action was taken.

In 1874 were presented two papers, one by L. Dunton,[6] of the Bridgewater (Mass.) Normal School; one by John Ogden,[7] of Ohio. These aroused sufficient interest to have a motion made that a committee be appointed for definite action, but the motion failed. During the next ten years there was a lull, save that three different years saw an attempt to do something, but in vain.

In 1885, A. R. Taylor,[8] principal of the State Normal School of Kansas, succeeded in securing the appointment of a committee. This became known as the "Chicago Com-

---

[1] N. E. A., 1863, p. 95.
[2] *Ibid.*, 1864, p. 179.
[3] *Ibid.*, 1865, p. 271.
[4] *Ibid.*, 1866, p. 135.
[5] *Ibid.*, 1871, pp. 73-79.
[6] *Ibid.*, 1874, pp. 234-245.
[7] *Ibid.*, 1874, pp. 216-229.
[8] *Ibid.*, 1885, p. 223.

mittee." In 1889, this committee made its final report on "Methods of Instruction and Courses of Instruction in Normal Schools." [1] This was so general in nature that it reached no definite conclusions. After a life of four years this committee died, leaving only a record of agitation.

In the next five years, 1890-1894, there was practically nothing done.

In 1895, Z. X. Snyder, of the Normal School at Greeley, Colo., secured the appointment of what became known the next year as the "Denver Committee." This committee worked for four years, and in 1899 made its report. Its chief contribution was the suggestion of six "centers" from which a good Normal School course could be derived. Genetic psychology is given one year's study.

In the year 1893, the well-known "Committee of Fifteen" was appointed by the department of superintendents. It reported in 1895. A sub-committee of five, all city superintendents, prepared a report on "The Training of Teachers." One question answered was, "To what extent should psychology be studied, and in what way?" The committee advocated the study of psychology as a basis for principles and methods. "Most fundamental and important of the professional studies which ought to be pursued by one intending to teach is psychology." [2]

The positive report of this committee, together with appended expressions from individual men of educational prominence, has doubtless had considerable influence in arousing more attention to this subject in the Normal Schools, some of which give considerable evidence of this.

Thus far, this chapter has tried to point out present practice as to requirements made of those preparing to teach,

[1] N. E. A., 1889, pp. 570-587.

[2] Report of Committee of Fifteen, p. 24.

as carried out in state examination systems and in curricula for intending teachers studying in universities and Normal Schools. Throughout, an emphasis has been found upon psychology.[1] This tradition and present practice is used as evidence—generally accepted—that psychology is an essential, a *sine qua non*, in the preparation of the teacher. Whatever truth there may be in this conclusion, the method would be considered wrong by Pearson. " It is imagination solving the universe, propounding a formula before the facts which the formula is to describe have been collected and classified. . . . Every few months we find, in one journal or another, some more or less brilliant hypothesis as to a novel factor in evolution; but how few are the instances in which this factor is accurately defined, or, being defined, a quantitative measure of its efficiency is obtained." [2]

[1] The development of this idea as to psychology is doubtless typical of that of any other subject in the Normal School course.

[2] Pearson, *Grammar of Science*, p. 373.

CHAPTER III

OPINIONS OF STUDENTS AS TO THE VALUE OF NORMAL SCHOOL PSYCHOLOGY

IT has elsewhere been pointed out that the Normal Schools have from the first emphasized the study of psychology by prospective teachers. This subject has appeared in the curriculum of every Normal School throughout the country. It has been tacitly assumed that the scientific or unscientific study of mind is a prerequisite to aiding in the developing of mind. Normal School instructors have looked to this subject as central in the course. Normal School students have usually had little, if any, choice in their work, and so have studied psychology without question. Patrons of the Normal School, and also the public schools, have usually been in sympathy with the Normal School practice.

The real question as to the pedagogical value of psychology has been little discussed. The question was, however, raised only two years after the founding of the Normal School. This was done by the editor of the American Institute of Instruction.[1] In a large number of articles in this periodical from the year of its founding, 1830 to 1899, the one article referred to is alone in calling in question the usually accepted value credited to this subject. In recent years Professor Münsterberg sounded a similar dissent in asserting that while psychology is a good educator, it has

---

[1] *American Institute of Instruction*, 1841, pp. 41-64.

no practical use in the hands of the teacher. Psychology is general, and cannot do justice to an individual case, as is demanded in teaching. Tact and sympathy are inhibited in the psychological teacher.[1] Dr. E. Harlow Russell, the head of one of the best known Normal Schools, while not agreeing with Professor Münsterberg, emphatically opposes the importance usually given to psychology.[2]

Just what psychology contributes to the individual teacher in her work is not easy to determine. It may even be impossible, and thus always remain a matter of personal judgment. Yet, a consensus of personal opinion cannot but contribute to the problem, even if not directly to the solution. A very limited questionnaire study has been made of the problem as to the contribution of psychology to efficiency in teaching. Many such studies have been published in the *Pedagogical Seminary*, and a few in the *American Journal of Psychology*. The methods there used have been rightly subjected to pointed criticisms.[3] 1. Much ignorance in reply to such questions is used as if it were wisdom, but "no research can ever retain a reliability beyond that possessed by the data with which it starts." 2. The facts reported are from a small and probably peculiar portion of the class involved, and hence are not representative. 3. The interpretation of the replies is largely a matter of personal opinion, and unless corrected by various checks, may lead to gross error. 4. "The progress from a set of statements about individuals to a statement about a group including them is by no means a matter of simple addition." Thus conclusions reached through such unscientific methods would be wholly unreliable.

[1] *Atlantic Monthly*, 85, p. 656 (May, 1900).

[2] Address before the New England Normal Council, May 15, 1903.

[3] Thorndike, *Educational Psychology*, pp. 152-162.

In the face of such plausible criticisms (with which I fully agree) a questionnaire study cannot be put forth for the purpose of conviction unless the above errors in method can be rendered harmless. In the present study, my use of the replies will be such as to make them at least of no great importance.

The conclusions from this questionnaire study do not, therefore, pretend to be proved facts, but are given only as hypotheses suggested by the study.

The purpose of this questionnaire was to get an estimate of the worth of psychology, as studied in Normal Schools, from the graduates of those schools now actively engaged in teaching. Questions were sent to graduates of all Normal Schools in Massachusetts save one, to all such schools in New York save two, and to a few schools in Pennsylvania and the Northwest. Questions were sent to four hundred and seventy-two persons, most of whom had graduated since 1897, and had had at least two years of experience. The following are the questions:

1. What did you feel to be the aim in the study of psychology?

2. What portions of psychology were most emphasized?

3. What text-books or works on psychology did you study or read?

4. Did you find in psychology principles for teaching? Please suggest one or more.

5. Which has helped you the more in your work, your study of psychology, or your study of principles and methods based on experience?

A total of one hundred and sixty-seven replies were received. Twenty-seven schools were represented in these replies. The replies to the individual questions are considered merely for their suggestiveness. It must be admitted at the outset that the number of replies considered is exceedingly small. A consensus of opinion really worth considering would probably ask for no fewer replies from each one of the twenty-seven schools. The individuals, however, to whom these questions were sent were selected wholly at random from lists furnished by the several schools. Thorndike, in his criticisms given above, points out that the questionnaire method is deficient on the ground that those who do reply are a special group, by reason of the desire either to oppose or support a suggested problem, while those without this desire do not trouble themselves in answering the questions asked. But in the case of the present questionnaire, those not replying would probably support, even more than those who did reply, the conclusions given below.

Upon the basis of this brief study, the following generalizations are made:

1. In the minds of those teaching, the work of psychology in the Normal Schools was very indefinite and unproductive.

2. The work done by the various schools, or by students in the same school, is not centered about a few principles, but is scattered.

3. The consensus of opinion is strongly in preference for experience rather than psychology as a contributing factor in their success as teachers.

4. Normal Schools where there is a special teacher of psychology give a more favorable impression of the value of the study of psychology.

5. The opinions concerning 3. summarized in this study are found inconsistent with the evidence on the same question, given by the historical point of view,[1] and also by the statistical study of the relation of psychology to teaching.[2] (However, this latter study, while showing that the correlations between scholarship in psychology and teaching

[1] See Chapter II.   [2] See Chapter IV.

efficiency is .418, does not assert that the whole other factor involved is experience.)

The question of greatest interest is the fifth. We are interested in the direct question as to whether the teacher is conscious of help from her study of psychology in the Normal School. The answers to the other questions, however, explain somewhat the positions taken with respect to the fifth.

The principle of apperception requires that only when a student " knows the purpose of the exercise do apperceiving ideas flow in rich fulness." That is, we expect a student to gain from his study of a subject in proportion as he knows the aim in the work. For this reason the first question was asked: " What did you feel to be the aim in the study of psychology?" To this question only 135 answers were made. This is only 81 per cent. of the whole number making replies, and only 29 per cent. of those to whom letters were sent. There are, however, representatives from every one of the 27 schools.

The answers are easily grouped as follows:

1. Knowledge of mind for the purpose of instruction.
2. Knowledge of mind as a scientific study.
3. " To understand the child."
4. Ethical development.
5. Special; *i. e.*, scattering answers.

Table I shows the distribution:

TABLE I

Answers.	*Number of Answers.*	*Per cent. of Replies to this Question.*	*Per cent. of Replies to Total Inquiries.*
1	76	56	16
2	26	19	6
3	11	8	2
4	4	3	1—
5	20	14	4

It is readily seen that the educational aspect has the

greatest prominence. Its interest is in its relation to the position taken on the fifth question considered below. It would be expected that the 56 per cent. who found this educational aim would also find pedagogical help in the work, but the answers to question five are to the contrary.

The chief interest in the answers to the second question (What portions of psychology were most emphasized?) is in what they do *not* contain—I mean in their lack of definiteness. The answers were too scattered to have meaning: *e. g.*, " Mental Development," " Fundamental Principles," " Principles of Teaching." Other answers covered an indefinite range: *e. g.*, " Mental Development," " Memory," " Attention," " Will," " Interest," " Imagination," all these in one answer. The leading conclusion, then, on this question is that no strong impression of one large and central thought, such as Herbart's apperception, or James' emphasis on native and acquired reactions, was made. The students left the school with many names of psychological topics in mind, and with no central thought.

Answers to the question on text-books show the chaotic condition of Normal School instruction in psychology. Forty-eight different books are mentioned. James, *Talks to Teachers* and *Briefer Course* (not distinguished), heads the list. Next in order are Halleck, Sully, Baldwin, (Joseph, I suspect,) Todd, Titchener, etc. Some books are mentioned that are not now regarded as of much pedagogical worth, *e. g.*, Haven, Porter, Hitchcock, Alden. Some replies show lack of knowledge as to what are psychologies by naming Laurie, Mann, McMurry, Rousseau.

The fourth question asked what principles for teaching were found in the study of psychology. A large number were given. Many were answers in a single word, and this not in all cases suggestive of a real principle. The following is the list of fifteen given in two or more of the answers:

		Number of votes	Value of votes
1.	Proceed from the Known to the Unknown.	37	22 +
2.	Association and Apperception	21	13 +
3.	Perception	18	12 +
4.	Habit	23	12 +
5.	Attention	18	8 +
6.	Interest	14	6 +
7.	Memory	11	5 +
8.	Order of Mental Development	8	5 +
9.	Self-activity	2	2
10.	Judgment	2	1 +
11.	Idea first, then the Name	2	1 +
12.	Proceed from the Whole to the Parts	2	1 —
13.	Proceed from the Particular to the General.	3	1 —
14.	First Impressions Are Strongest	3	1 —
15.	Proceed from the Easy to the Difficult	2	1 —

Only 109 replies were made to this question, *i. e.*, 65 per cent. of total answers, and 23 per cent. of the inquiries made. The question of importance here is the emphasis laid upon the various so-called principles. Some mentioned one only; others gave several. It is unjust to count each principle suggested as one. The problem is essentially that of counting the ballots of voters who had the privilege of voting for any number they pleased. But in voting for more than one they thereby split their vote. Thus, one who cast five ballots gave to each of such candidates one-fifth of a vote.

The list above shows the results by two methods. The first column of figures shows the total of 195 ballots cast for the various " candidates." The second column of figures shows the result when each candidate received only his share when a ballot was split. The relative rank is thus slightly changed. Here it is seen that the " Proceed from the Known to the Unknown " " covers a multitude of sins." It is one of the indefinite statements so characteristic of all the answers. Secondly, it is evident that the Normal School psychology in the various schools is not emphasizing a few, but many diverse, principles.

The fifth question is the most direct and important one: " Which has helped you more in your work, your study of psychology, or your study of principles and methods, based on experience?"

The total number of answers to this question was 143, *i. e.*, 85 per cent. of all answers given and 30 per cent. of inquiries made.   The distribution is as follows:

	Answers.	*Per cent. of total.*		*Per cent, of 114.*
In favor of experience....	87	61	(71%)	76
In favor of psychology....	27	19	(29%)	24
The two not separated....	29	20		

There is evidence here of a strong emphasis upon experience as more helpful than psychology.   The 71 and 29 per cents. express the ratio when the answers of the 29, who do not separate experience and psychology, are evenly divided.   The more equitable method, however, is to discard in this treatment these 29.   This gives 76 and 24 as the percentages of the positive answers for experience and psychology.   The question as stated may be interpreted as referring to psychology as a subject independent of the Normal School.   It is perfectly possible that many of the answers are upon this basis.   However, there is evidence that it was not so considered in the answers.   Again, most of the answers are given by teachers who have been out of the Normal School less than five years, and they give no evidence of studying much psychology in that time.   Again, as will be shown, there are a large number of positive references to the psychology as studied in the school.   The ratio in favor of experience is of even more weight than indicated by the figures, when, as referred to above, it is remembered that the answers—in large measure—are from those with quite limited experience.   This want of experience gives an advantage, if anything, to the side of psychology.

It is of interest and profit to note the impression made by a few individual schools. It seems natural to expect that those schools having special teachers in psychology would impress their students with the importance of psychology; whereas, in those schools in which the subject is given by the principal of the school, with a much more general treatment, much less may be expected.

Table II, *A* and *B*, shows the schools having special teachers of psychology, and those having none, respectively. (Schools 23 to 29 are omitted, since there seems to be no definite field of psychology distinct from pedagogy.) At the side of the school list is indicated the number favoring experience or psychology. A marked contrast is seen at once. In those schools having special teachers of psychology, 35½ per cent. favor psychology; while in the other class of schools, the per cent. is reduced to 10. In group *A*, only one school, No. 20, gives evidence which might have been expected of schools with special teachers. Yet this weight is somewhat lessened when it is known that of the seven who directly favor psychology, three are teachers of psychology; one as principal of a Normal School, one at the head of this department in a Normal School, the third as teacher of a city training class. A similar disposition can be made of three of the seven in school No. 11. In group *A* are only three schools in which those favoring psychology equal their opponents in number, and in two of these cases they exceed. In group *B*, six schools have none in favor of the psychology studied; and the other four schools have only one representative each on this side. Thus, even in those schools where much might be expected in emphasis upon psychology, little support is found, and much less by the other group.

Some characteristic replies of individuals throw a decided light upon the impression Normal School psychology has made upon those who have pursued the work.

TABLE II

PSYCHOLOGY VS. EXPERIENCE

School.	Experience.	Psychology.	Both.*
1	5	1	1
2	1		
3		2	1
4	3		2
5	4	1	1
6	1		
8	1	1	2
9	3	2	3
10	4		1
11	16	7	1
14	8		
16	5		
18	4	1	2
19	3		
20	3	7	4
21	1	1	1
22	7	1	1
23	1		2
24	3		2
25		1	
26	3		
28	1		
29	2		
37	2		2
38	2	1	1
39	6	1	2
	87 = 76 %	27 = 24 %	29

A

From schools with special teachers of psychology.

School.	Experience.	Psychology.	Both.*
3		2	1
6	1		
8	1	1	2
9	3	2	3
10	4		1
11	16	7	1
18	4	1	2
20	3	7	4
38	2	1	1
39	6	1	2
	40 = 64½ %	22 = 35½ %	17

B

From schools without special teachers of psychology.

School.	Experience.	Psychology.	Both.*
1	5	1	1
2	1		
4	3		2
5	4	1	1
14	8		
16	5		
19	3		
21	1	1	1
22	7	1	1
37	2		2
	39 = 90 + %	4 = 10 — %	8

*This means that the answers took the position that the two are inseparable. These are not considered in the percentages given.

" Psychology gave a rationale for all that experience taught. It enabled me to profit by experience. . . . Through psychology I gained a criterion of value." Essentially the same thought is expressed by two others (all three of these are Normal School instructors). A very few speak of psychology as having been to them of a general value—a basis for interpretations, a means of awakening mental activities, etc. A few, in favoring experience, speak of it as based in a general way upon psychology. Only one reply makes an attempt to state specifically and concretely results gained from the work in psychology. This reply is from a school known for its special strength in this department.

On the other hand is the emphatic position taken by those replying against psychology. Many of the answers are accompanied by the expressions, " most decidedly," " emphatically," etc., none of which are used favoring psychology. " A waste of time " is used to express the general results of the work. No greater criticism is given upon the content of the work than in its being constantly characterized as " indefinite." This indefiniteness is indicated by those who speak in support of the work in psychology, as well as those who condemn it. Illustrative of the former is " My study of psychology taught me to study the child from a psychological standpoint;" others speak directly of getting very little that was definite. In the second case, this indefiniteness is even more strongly indicated; for example, the work in psychology " began nowhere and ended in the same place;" or, the work was " an harrassing blind groping after something intangible;" again, even the instructor " did not know what he was doing."

Many answers point out that the work was " not psychology at all, but philosophy of education." And this is clearly seen in the study of text-books reported. Others speak of the "very superficial study of psychology," and characterize it further as "old." A number of these answers are from college graduates, who have later pursued the Normal School course. Most of these express dissatisfaction with the work done in psychology. By these reference is made to "the much larger and more helpful amount" received elsewhere. A representative of one of the leading Normal Schools—and now himself a principal—takes a position which well expresses the real tendency and chief emphasis in the answers to this question. He says that in the Normal School, experience was of more value to him, but that since leaving the school, psychology has taken the lead. It is interesting to note, also, that the strongest expressions of adverse criticism come from representatives of three schools ranked among the highest, all of which have special teachers of psychology.

There may be more scientific tests of the worth of any subject, but the impression which such a study makes upon a random selection of individuals who have pursued that work is an indication of how it *is* valued, if not of how it *ought* to be.

The answers to our question as to the relative value of psychology and experience in Normal School work suggest, in brief, the following:

1. The work in psychology has favorably impressed only a small minority—24 per cent.—and only a few of these speak specifically in commendation of the work.

2. The most favorable impression made is in the "general value" of the study—a "brain stretcher," as expressed by one. But this suggests:

3. Characteristic weakness in its indefiniteness. The work fails to bring forth results that show clearly to those who take it.

4. The work is more in name than in reality. Some re-

plies state that there was no psychology given, though the subject does appear in the curriculum. The psychology—so-called—is superficial and " old," or is only a name for the " Philosophy of Education."

5. The work falls below that given in college, as testified by college graduates; and further, below that which will be obtained in practical work in teaching.

6. Finally, the contrast between the schools having special teachers of psychology and those having none is marked. In the former class, roughly, a third favor psychology, while in the latter there is less than one in ten.

It is, perhaps, unnecessary to call the reader's attention, in closing this chapter, to the fact that all its contents concern, not real psychology as it might be taught in Normal Schools, but the thing which has been taught under the name of psychology. Nor should the reader conclude that the obvious inadequacy of psychology as taught implies a greater worth in other Normal School subjects. On the contrary, there is reason to believe that the other subjects would have fared as badly if similarly tested by a questionnaire of the same sort.

CHAPTER IV

ON THE CORRELATION BETWEEN TEACHING EFFI-
CIENCY AND SCHOLARSHIP

Introduction

1. The Problem.

Chapter II showed how one particular subject in the curriculum came to be considered necessary in the training of teachers. Chapter III showed the inadequacy of the instruction in one sample subject of the Normal School curriculum. The present chapter proposes to study, by a statistical and scientific method, the relation between teaching efficiency and scholarship in various subjects pursued in preparation for teaching.

This is the problem: Is the efficient teacher the proficient scholar? To what extent is he so in each of the subjects of the Normal School course? In other words, does the one who stands high among fellow-teachers stand relatively high among fellow-students in the work preparatory to his teaching? Such a study of mental relationships is in itself a study of causes. If it be found a rule that efficiency in teaching follows proficiency in scholarship, then, other things being equal, the latter may be considered a vital contribution to the former. And this is our present purpose: to discover, so far as possible, what elements enter into the making of a capable teacher. Corollary questions are: To what extent does proficiency in scholarship mean efficiency in teaching? That is, what is the quantitative relation? This involves the measurement of scholarship in the various subjects pursued; and the question of the relation of these measurements among themselves arises. Again, what do the details of the data suggest as to the character of the measurements used?

This study is confined to elementary teachers only; that is, those below the high school.[1] A study of high school teachers would probably give different results, since there can be little doubt that scholarship enters more directly into the success of the high school teacher, who usually deals more with particular subject-matter and less with general human nature than the teacher in the elementary school.

This study, also, does not attempt to ascertain fully just what *does* constitute teaching efficiency. Of the many possible factors—health, personality, favorable environment, etc.—which determine success in teaching, only one, ability in academic and professional studies, is investigated. The present study seeks the relations between (1) those mental traits which are measured by Normal School records of scholarship, and (2) the *ability to teach* as measured by one who allows for favorable or unfavorable conditions.

2. *General Conclusions Reached.*

The more important general conclusions reached in this study may be briefly stated as follows:

1. The correlations [2] found are low. Taking together the 92 relationships calculated herein between teaching efficiency and scholarship in various subjects, the narrow mode, that point in the series containing the greatest number of

---

[1] The data studied include one exception, viz., School F, but these marks are considered separately.

[2] The reader unacquainted with the modern methods of estimating relationships should read the chapters on "Correlation" in Bowley's *Elements of Statistics*, Davenport's *Statistical Methods*, or Thorndike's *Mental and Social Measurements*.

frequencies, is at the zero point, which means no correlation. Widen this mode so that it will include half the cases, and it then lies between .000 and .337, with the median at .175. When we consider that the Normal Schools are strictly technical schools—or at least so intended—this low correlation between the theory as given in the school and the art as practiced outside is rather surprising.

2. The relation between the practice teaching within the school and actual teaching outside the training school is comparatively high, *viz.*, .443.

3. The data lend support to the claim so generally made, especially in Normal Schools, that the ability developed in the study of psychology contributes much to one's success in teaching. This subject stands next to that of practice teaching, *viz.*, .418. This is in accord with the opinion and experience of Normal School instructors from the first impulse made by Cyrus Pierce in Lexington (1839) to the present. But, as shown in Chapter II, the study of psychology has been constantly mingled with the history and principles of education, independently of which it cannot be well considered. Hence, in this study, consideration is given to these various studies combined, called " Professional." As such, the correlation is lowered to .336, but still ranks second.

4. The question as to the relative value of studies in subject-matter itself, and studies in the methods of teaching such subjects, receives a suggestion. In fourteen pairs of such relations studied, ten result in favor of the academic, *i. e.*, the subject-matter work. The differences, however, are slight, as indicated in the following figures. These figures express in thousandths the differences in the coefficients of correlation in favor of academic work: .043, .099, .039, .030, .020, .137, .059, .246, .193, .084. The differences in

favor of methods are: .054, .052, .149, .072.   In one of
the city training schools there is evidence to this same effect.
Examinations also show that ability in academic subjects
contributes more to successful teaching than ability in
courses in methods.

5. The question of the efficiency of examinations as tests
of ability to teach was studied.   The results, however, are
not satisfactory, because of the peculiar data used.   But, so
far as the present study goes, the evidence is against the
efficiency of examinations as tests of ability to teach.   In
two schools considered, the correlations between teaching
efficiency and examination records are distinctly negative.
In the third school the coefficient is below .20.

6. The order in closeness of relationship to teaching efficiency of the four branches of study, considered in two
aspects, academic and methods, is as follows:

English	Methods.
Science	"
History	Academic.
English	"
Mathematics	Methods.
Science	Academic.
Mathematics	"
History	Methods.

These are the leading conclusions as to the correlations
calculated.   In this study the question of marking, *i. e.*,
grading, could not be entirely avoided.   The systems of
marking used in the various schools indicate carelessness in
this particular and a need of improvement in method.   This
is discussed at the close of the chapter, and suggestions are
given for another system of measuring mental traits.

This inaccuracy in grading, both in the subjects studied
and in teaching efficiency, results in an " attenuation " of
all the coefficients of correlation, as has been shown by

Spearman.[1] As the data for this study were gathered before his paper had shown the need of two independent measures for every trait to be related, I am not able to correct my results for the attenuations due to chance error. There is no reason to believe that the *relative* closeness of relationship to teaching efficiency of the different abilities measured would be altered if the Spearman correction could be made.

METHOD OF STUDY

1. *Data Collected.*

The materials used consist of records of teachers from the following institutions:

1. Five representative Normal Schools of Massachusetts and New York:

  School A—155 graduates.
    " B—105   "
    " C— 55   "
    " D— 89   "
    " E—102   "

2. Two Normal Colleges.

  School F— 45 graduates.
    " G— 97   "

3. Two city training schools.

  School H—157 graduates.
    " I— 52   "

4. One educational department of a university.

  School J—222 students.

5. Three Ohio cities.

  School K—106 teachers.

Total number of individuals studied—1,185.

[1] *American Journal of Psychology*, Jan., 1904.

The following table (III) shows the subjects in which marks have been secured in the various schools. For example, the Y in column *A* opposite Psychology indicates that I have records of individual students in Psychology at school A. The Math. Ac., Science Ac., *etc.*, indicate academic work in these four branches, distinct from the usual method work given in Normal Schools. Grades in both phases are used in this investigation. The term " Education " found in schools B and C means History of Education, Philosophy of Education, School Economy, *etc.*, given in one course as found in some Normal Schools, or not easily distinguished here. It would, however, doubtless be safe to consider these two cases as History of Education in comparisons made, and I have so done in the calculations. The marks for Mathematics, Science, History, and English are made up from marks in the individual subjects in these branches, *e. g.*, Mathematics includes Arithmetic, Algebra, Geometry. The last five branches mentioned refer to academic work preparatory to the work in the training school. The marks in school K are upon local examinations for teachers' certificates. The number of marks in the various subjects taken and upon teaching will average about twenty for each individual. This means about 25,000 (over 24,-000) records used in this investigation.

TABLE III

Schools	A	B	C	D	E	F	G	H	I	J	K
Teaching	Y	Y	Y	Y	Y	Y					
" Instruction.							Y	Y			
" Discipline..							Y	Y			
City Exam.											
" Hist. Prin.							Y	Y			
" Methods							Y	Y			
" Total..........							Y	Y			
Practice Teach.	Y		Y	Y		Y		Y	Y	Y	
Psychology	Y	Y	Y	Y	Y	Y		Y	Y	Y	
Educ. Psy.										Y	
Hist. of Ed.	Y			Y	Y	Y		Y	Y	Y	
"Education"...... .		Y	Y								Y
Mathematics.......	Y	Y	Y	Y	Y	Y		Y		Y	
Math. Ac.		Y	Y	Y							
Science	Y	Y	Y	Y	Y	Y		Y		Y	
Science Ac.........		Y	Y	Y							
History............	Y	Y	Y	Y	Y	Y		Y		Y	
History Ac.		Y	Y	Y							
English	Y	Y	Y	Y	Y	Y		Y		Y	
English Ac.		Y	Y	Y							
Art			Y		Y						
Man. Train.			Y		Y						
Gymnastics					Y						
Academic work prior to training school work.											
Mathematics.......								Y			Y
Science								Y			Y
History............								Y			Y
English								Y			Y
Mod. Lang.								Y			

2. *Character of Data.*

It must be frankly admitted at the outset that a strictly scientific treatment of the problem in hand is handicapped by the very nature of the data used. We have a strictly quantitative measure for land in the " foot-front " or acre, for coal in the ton or car-load. These are absolute measures and are universal. Not so in the measurement of scholarship or teaching efficiency. These are mental traits

to which physical measurements do not apply.   Yet in
almost all phases of educational work amounts of mentality
are commonly expressed in some form of units of measure.
Examinations are marked 98%, 86%, 37%, *etc.*; or by letters A, B, B—, C, C—, D, *etc.*; or by numbers 1, 2, 3, *etc.*;
or by words "excellent," "good," "poor," *etc.*   Various
are the terms used, not only in examinations, but in daily
recitations, in written work of all forms, as symbols of
impressions of teaching efficiency and of general scholarship.

These "marks" are commonly accepted as good measures, and they are commonly understood.   Only in critical
cases are these marks called in question, when it is seen
that the same "mark" given by different individuals does
not measure the same amount of mentality.   98% given
by one teacher may mean the same as 86% given by another; an "A" student under one instructor is only a "B"
student as marked by another.   Further, and as a conse-
quence of what has just been said, any "mark" is not a
measure of the student's *absolute* mental ability, but is
rather an expression of an individual's estimate of that
ability.   It is, in the last analysis, a personal opinion, rather
than a universal measure.

Yet, in spite of these real difficulties, we had best use
"marks," for they are practically the only available measures at present of mentality.   This investigation makes use
of such "marks," though tentatively, as approximations to
true measures of ability, if treated as determining the order
of merit.   Conclusions reached from such data will be subject to less criticism by reason of the two facts mentioned,
viz., these "marks" are commonly accepted as an adequate
measure, and these "marks" are commonly understood,
though not with great accuracy.   Time and experience may
develop a standard of measurement of various mental traits,
as the foot and ton in physical measurements.

3. Method of Securing Data.

1. Marks for teaching efficiency.

There are very few school systems where we find the teachers graded on the efficiency of their work. (This is done in practice work in training schools, but seldom in actual school work.) If each principal or superintendent marked his teachers, as these teachers mark their pupils, we would have at hand an estimate of the teaching power of each. But such is not the case. Any attempt to secure this estimate from the principals of 1,185 teachers scattered throughout three states or more, or to inquire into the actual work done by these teachers, would be an almost insurmountable task. Another method was taken. Principals of Normal Schools usually follow quite closely the work of their graduates. The estimate of such men is probably the best available mark for teaching efficiency. This is the mark used in this study.

In selecting the individuals, the roll of classes graduating between 1898 and 1902, inclusive, was taken. The individuals were taken in order, in so far as the principal of the school had followed the work of the graduate sufficiently to be ready to estimate the efficiency of the teaching. All others were discarded.

The above method was used for schools A-F, inclusive. For the graduates of schools G and H, marks are given by the principals of the schools in which such graduates are teaching. I have no records of the teaching of graduates of schools I and J. Their practice teaching only was available. Marks for school K were given by the superintendents of the three schools respectively.

2. Marks for scholarship.

These marks were secured for each of the 1,185 indi-

---

[1] Mental and Physical Tests, *Psy. Rev. Monograph*, iii, no. 6, p. 35.

viduals in the various subjects pursued in the schools, or upon examination. As already said, the mark in Mathematics is the combined marks of whatever subjects are found in that branch. In most of the Normal Schools, these are Arithmetic, Algebra, Geometry. This combined mark is not the exact " average " of the other marks, but is rather the probable " mode," which is a truer mark.[1]

NOTE.—Wissler, in considering students' marks in Columbia University, takes as the standing for the year the " sum of the products of the grades and the number of course hours divided by the total number of such hours, or the average grade per course hours." [1] While this method of exact average is doubtless well used in this case, the "mode" seems preferable where the marks cover a wider range and are less regular.

4. *Method of Treatment.*

(1) Coefficients of correlation.

With these " marks " as measures of intellectual powers in various subjects of study and of efficiency in teaching, the question is as to their relations, particularly the relation between teaching efficiency and scholarship in the various branches of study. If the work of the Normal Schools and teachers' colleges is to equip the individual for efficient teaching, it is important to know what subjects of study contribute to this end, and to what relative extent they do so. This calls for measurements of specific mental powers, and of the extent to which an individual's station in one corresponds to his station in others.

This is done by a method based on that of Pearson's coefficient of correlation.[2] This method is not one of abso-

---

[1] Thorndike, *Educational Psychology*, 166, and *Lecture Notes*, 1903-1904.

[2] This method is fully described in Pearson's *Grammar of Science*, pp. 392-402; also in Thorndike's *Educational Psychology* and his *Mental and Social Measurements.*

lute amount of condition or of change. It is a measure of mental relationship, of the amount of excess or deficiency in relation to the central tendency of various relationships. The index or coefficient of correlation marks the degree of relationship. This may vary from $+ 100\%$, which is perfect correspondence, to -100%, which is perfect opposition. "A correlation of $+62\%$ would mean that . . . any given station in the one trait would imply 62 hundredths of that station in the other. A coefficient of -62% would, of course, mean that any degree of superiority would involve 62 hundredths as much inferiority, and *vice versa*." [1] This only means that the higher the correlation, the more certain we can be that high scholarship in the given subject is essential in efficient teaching; that a given efficiency in one is connected with proficiency in the other to the extent indicated by the index of correlation. Pearson speaks of the increase in correlation as the " transition of correlation into causation. Causation tells us that B will accompany A; correlation tells us the proportion of cases in which B accompanies." [2]

One statement only needs to be made as to the method of securing the index of correlation. The Pearson coefficient is obtained by the following process: [3] Find the sum of the products of the deviations of one class by the deviations associated therewith in the other class; divide this sum by the product of the Standard Deviation of one class multiplied by the Standard Deviation of the other class, multiplied by the whole number of cases. This is expressed by the formula:

---

[1] Thorndike, *Mental and Social Measurements*, p. 123.

[2] *Grammar of Science*, p. 397.

[3] See Pearson's *Grammar of Science*, p. 400; Davenport, *Statistical Methods*, p. 32; Thorndike, *Educational Psychology*. p. 26.

$$r = \frac{\Sigma x.y}{n\sigma_1\sigma_2}$$

The deviations have in all cases been calculated according to the hypothesis that the *relative position* of individuals marked by the same person is given by their marks, and that the distributions of the abilities studied approximate the so-called normal type. The *amounts* of the marks thus have no influence more than to determine within any one school the *relative* abilities of the individuals. The second part of this hypothesis is by no means secure, but any other way of treating the marks would make little difference in the resulting coefficients of correlation.

The large amount of arithmetical work required in finding $\Sigma x.y$, σ_1, and σ_2, is much lessened by a transmutation table given by Professor Thorndike.[1] By this method the following (Table IV) is an illustration of the treatment of each correlation. The top line of the table proper, exclusive of the figures in italics, reads: The 40 students ranking highest in scholarship in professional studies ranked in teaching efficiency as follows: 17 in the highest group, 14 in the next highest, 4 in the third, 4 in the fourth and 1 in the lowest group.

TABLE IV

TEACHING EFFICIENCY

Scholarship in		1	2	3	4	5	Totals	Per cent		$\sigma/100$
Professional	*1*	17	14	4	4	1	40	=	9	+181
Studies	*2*	20	20	14	4		58	=	13	+103
	3	24	47	27	14	6	118	=	25	+ 41
	4	12	40	38	14	8	112	=	24	− 23
	5	10	20	30	11	5	76	=	16	− 82
	6	5	7	11	7	7	37	=	8	−135
	7	3	4	9	8	1	25	=	5	−210
Totals		91	152	133	62	28	466			
Per cent.		20	33	28	13	6				
Stand. Dev.		+140	+36	−45	−117	−199				

[1] *Mental and Social Measurements*, pp. 89-94.

The products are :

			$+$	$-$
17 $\times$ $+140$ $\times$	$+181$ $=$	430780		
20	$+103$ $=$	288400		
24	$+$ 41 $=$	137760		
12	$-$ 23 $=$			38640
10	$-$ 82 $=$			114800
5	-135 $=$			94500
3	-210 $=$			88200
14 $\times$ $+$ 36 $\times$	$+181$ $=$	91224		
20	$+103$ $=$	74160		
47	$+$ 41 $=$	69372		
40	$-$ 23 $=$			33120
20	$-$ 82 $=$			59040
7	-135 $=$			34020
4	-210 $=$			30240
4 $\times$ $-$ 45 $\times$	$+181$ $=$			32580
14	$+103$ $=$			64890
27	$-$ 41 $=$			44280
38	$-$ 23 $=$	39330		
30	$-$ 82 $=$	110700		
11	-135 $=$	66825		
9	-210 $=$	85050		
4 $\times$ -117 $\times$	$+181$ $=$			84708
4	$+103$ $=$			48204
14	$+$ 41 $=$			67158
14	$-$ 23 $=$	37674		
11	$-$ 82 $=$	105534		
7	-135 $=$	110565		
8	-210 $=$	196560		
1 $\times$ -199 $\times$	$+181$ $=$			36019
6	$+$ 41 $=$			48954
8	$-$ 23 $=$	36616		
5	$-$ 82 $=$	81590		
7	-135 $=$	188055		
1	-210 $=$	41790		
			2191985	919353
			919353	

$$466)1272632(273$$

$$r = .273$$
$$\text{P. E. of } r = .027$$
$$n = 466$$

NOTE—The above calculations are such that the products should show four decimal places. These have been inserted in the final result.

The above method has been followed in the one hundred and twenty tables used. In a few tables the group method has been used to save difficulties and to avoid errors which would probably have been greater than by the method used. The method without grouping is probably the more accurate, since it gives more attention to individual cases. The difference, however, is very slight; for example, in one table the two methods bring as the index of correlation .209 and .208. In the few groupings made, care was taken to group about the centre and avoid any such changes at the extremes.

(2) Method of combining schools.

It is already apparent that the method used in this study is that of working out individual correlations in various schools. In so doing, the measure of relationship (indicated by the index of correlation) between any two abilities is found to vary in the different schools. For example, the indices of correlation between efficiency in teaching and the " professional " work in the Normal Schools are .273, .431, .018, .241, .568. This difference is due to the difference in the number of cases used in each, to different standards of marking in the various schools, to actual differences in the relation; and there may be other causes. It would, doubtless, be desirable to use data drawn from all these schools subjected to the same measurements in each of the two characteristics compared. This is obviously impossible, since the ratings for each individual considered must come from his own school. We have no " rule " to measure the mental stature of all. In another section [1] of this chapter the averages of these various relations have been worked out, which may stand as representing the relation between

---

[1] Pages 71, 72.

any two traits studied. These averages are of the indices only, as indicated on pages 71, 72. Another method which might have been used is that of combining the whole number of cases in the various schools. This is used in the illustration of method on pages 65-67.

The use of the percentage system in grading may be properly considered as a marking by relative positions. For example, if the marks in a given school in a particular class have a range from 59 per cent. to 96 per cent., we may regard the class as divided into 38 groups, arranged in consecutive order, from the best to the poorest in the trait thus measured. As said above, not all the grades between 59 and 96 may be used. In that case, the number of groups is reduced by the number of grades omitted. Did all schools use a system of grading that would give the same number of groups in each class thus rated, to combine the marks of the different schools would be simple. For example, the grades in arithmetic in two given classes may be as follows:

    (1) 96, 93, 91, 90, 89, 88, 85, 80, 78, 75, 68, 65.
    (2) 98, 95, 92, 90, 88, 85, 82, 80, 70, 65, 60, 50.
Rank 1, 2, 3, 4, 5, 6, 7, 8, 9, 10, 11, 12.
and be thus divided into twelve groups according to relative position. The individual (or individuals) in school (1) who stands 93 has the same relative position as the individual in school (2) who stands 95; that is, both stand second highest in the class. In such case, the measures in the two schools are easily comparable: by transposing the given grades to the standing in relative position, indicated by the series 1 to 12.

In case one school used twice as many grades as the other, two grades may be combined in one rank. For example,

(3) 96, 90, 85, 82, 80, 78, 75, 70.
(4) 98, 92, 85, 80, 75, 65, 60, 50.
    95, 89, 82, 77, 70, 62, 55, 40.
Rank 1, 2, 3, 4, 5, 6, 7, 8.

That is, school (4) has used a group system of twice the number used by school (3). A larger unit of measure (in this case 8 groups instead of 16) will place 98 and 95 in the first rank, 92 and 89 in the second rank, *etc.* It may seem that the bunching should be at the centre—the mode representing the central tendency—since here a slight change has less effect, and this will be used to some extent shortly. But when we consider the relative position only, and apply a larger unit of measure, the 98 and 95 seem to belong to the first class; so 50 and 40 to the lowest class.

In case, however, the number of groups in one is not an exact multiple of the other, a somewhat different method is to be used. Here a partial grouping at the centre is to play a part. That is, so far as possible, the groups of the larger are to be evenly combined to correspond to the series of a smaller number of groups. But whenever inequality is to exist, the central groups are to receive the more. The following, taken from the data for A6, B6, C6, D6, E6, is an example:

School E (5 groups)	1	2	3	4	5
" D (5 ")	1	2	3	4	5
" A (10 ")	1.2	3.4	5.6	7.8	9.10
" C (8 ")	1	2.3	4.5	6.7	8
" B (18 ")	1-3	4-7	8-11	12-15	16-18.

The bunching at the centre may be illustrated by the following, taken from tables 1A, 1B, 1C, 1E:

School E (5 groups)	1	2	3	4	5
" C (8 ")	1	2	3-6	7	8
" B (17 ")	1	2	3-15	16	17
" A (10 ")	1	2	3-8	9	10.

The two methods of grouping give practically no differences in results, *e. g.*, the index of correlation in a sample case (see Table V) is .288 by the former method and .296 by the latter. Comparing the indices obtained from grouped results with the average indices from the five schools, we find the former slightly higher.

TABLE V

TABLE I ABCE

	1	2	3	4	5	
1	10	11	7			28
2	16	21	4	3		44
3	12	30	13	7	1	63
4	21	42	77	17	5	162
5	2	5	18	11	4	40
6		4	7	2	5	18
7	10	11	8	11	4	44
	71	124	134	51	19	399

r = .288

TABLE I ABCE(1)

	1	2	3	4	5	
1	9	8	5			22
2	11	12	7	1		31
3	6	17	18	1		42
4	13	17	195	7	3	235
5	2		11	4	3	20
6		1	8	2	1	12
7	9	5	16	6	1	37
	50	60	260	21	8	399

r = .296

(3) Tables of distribution.

The tables of distribution are in themselves of much importance. For example, compare the facts for schools **A** and D in teaching and " professional."

The arrays are as follows, expressed in percentage of the total number of cases :

In teaching—
School A—4, 7, 22, 16, 20, 19, 6, 3, 3, 1.
    "   D—16, 16, 36, 2, 5, 4, 4, 2, 8, 2, 4.

In " professional "—
School A—1, 3, 2, 2, 3, 4, 3, 6, 5, 17, 4, 5, 9, 7, 6, 4, 4.
    "   D—32, 21, 21, 13, 13.

It is evident in the first two arrays that school D marks teaching efficiency much higher than school A, while in the second group of arrays, the characteristic difference is the scale of marking: school A makes close distinctions, while school D covers only a short range, making but five groups.

Interpretation and Discussion of Results

1. General Explanation of Tables and Tabular View of Indices.

The following are the correlations made:[1]

No. 1. Teaching and Psychology.
" 2. " " History and Principles of Education.
" 3. " " "Professional" (No. 1 and No. 2).
" 4. " " Practice Teaching.
" 5. " " Mathematics.
" 5-1. " " " (academic).
" 5-2. " " " (secondary).
" 6. " " Science.
" 6-1. " " " (academic).
" 6-2. " " " (secondary).
" 7. " " History.
" 7-1. " " " (academic).
" 7-2. " " " (secondary).
" 8. " " English.
" 8-1. " " " (academic).
" 8-2. " " " (secondary).
" 9. " " Modern Language (secondary).
" 10. " " "Methods" (5, 6, 7, 8).
" 11. " " "Academic" (5-1, 6-1, 7-1, 8-1).
" 12. " " Practice Teaching and "Methods."
" 13. " " Practice Teaching and Academic.
" 14. " " General Average.
" 15. " " Art.
" 16. " " Manual Training.

[1] For indices of correlation, see tabular view in Table VI.

No. 17. Teaching and Gymnasium.
" 18. " " City Examination in Methods.
" 19. " " City Examination in History and Principles of Education.
" 20. " " " Total " (18, 19).
" 21. Practice Teaching and Psychology.
" 22. " " " Educational Psychology.
" 23. " " " Psychology and Educational Psychology.
" 24. " " " History and Principles of Education.
" 25. " " " " Professional " (21, 22, 24).
" 26. " " " Mathematics.
" 27. " " " Science.
" 28. " " " History.
" 29. " " " English.
" 30. " " " " Methods " (26-29).
" 31. " Professional " and " Methods."
" 32. Average in Secondary Schools and Average in Training Schools.
" 33. Average in Secondary Schools and Average in City Examinations.
" 34. Average in Training Schools and Average in City Examinations.
" 35. " Professional " and Average in City Examinations.
" 36. " Instruction " and " Discipline."
" 37. A, B, C, E. Teaching and Psychology (four schools combined).
" 38. A, B, C, E. Teaching and Psychology (four schools combined).
" 39. A-E. Teaching and " Professional " five schools combined).

The seven different schools, or groups of teachers studied, are designated by letters A, B, etc., to J. Thus, 4 D is the correlation between teaching and practice teaching in school D. Most of the measures of scholarship are in terms of the old standard per cent. mark, ranging from 100 downward. Not all these are consecutive, since in a group of one hundred individuals some may be graded 86, 87, 90, 91, but none 88, 89. These breaks in the series do not interfere with the method, which emphasizes relative position rather than absolute standing. School D uses 1, 2, 3, in all grades except the mark for teaching efficiency. Other schools use letters A, B, C, etc. These mark relative positions only. In such schools these marks take the place of percents in the series. Still another form is used in some of the series: *e. g.*, 1-2, 2-3, A-B, B-C. These result from making averages of two or more marks. For example, the average of grades 1 and 2 give the grade 1-2; of B and C, the grade B-C. School H has a special mark used, which will be explained when that table is studied (see page 99).

In table VI is given a tabular view of the indices of correlation for the various relations studied in the different schools designated by the letters at the top. In each case the index is expressed in thousandths. The few cases of negative correlation are expressed by the — sign.

In column X is given the averages of the several schools taken together in the various subjects. These averages are obtained by weighting the individual indices according to the number of cases studied in each. An approximation for the various schools gives the following relation of weight:[1] A, 3; B, 2; C. 1; D, 2; E, 2; F, 1; G, 1; H, 3; I, 1; J, 3.
Thus, in number 1 we have:

[1] See number of cases per school, p. 55.

	Not Weighted	Weight	Weighted
A ················	332	3	996
B ················	417	2	834
C ················	004	1	004
E ················	546	2	1092

The average of the not-weighted is 325; of the weighted, 366. The difference is but little, but the latter is taken to be nearer the true average. Vacant places in the tabular view indicate the absence of the marks needed for such correlations in those schools.

TABLE VI

Table Number.	Subjects correlated with Teaching.	A	B	C	D	E	F	G	H	I	J	K	X	Y	Z
1	Psychology	332	417	004	000	546							366	366	418
2	Hist. & Prin. of Education	209	374	-039	233	495	-139						241	279	314
3	"Professional"	273	431	018	241	568			002				256	331	366
4	Practice Teaching	438		100	451		465		025				285	386	443
	Mathematics														
5	Methods	221	250	-116	010	310	279		084				158	168	200
5-1	Academic		293	-017	049								133	133	171
5-2	Preparatory Exam.								114			280			
	Science														
6	Methods	361	271		120	402	015		037				215	297	297
6-1	Academic		217	009	140								145	145	179
6-2	Preparatory Exam.								274			124			
	History														
7	Methods	004	383		-130	349			013				105	164	164
7-1	Academic		442	051	116								233	233	279
7-2	Preparatory Exam.								206			095			
	English														
8	Methods	353	473	030	135	453	304		044				261	321	353
8-1	Academic		381	-119	151								189	189	266
8-2	Preparatory Exam.								-028			225			
9	Modern Language								118						
10	"Methods"	290	423	-025	140	473	241		088				245	291	327
11	"Academic"		420	009	035				213				219	224	277
12	Practice Teach. & Meth.	359		054	293		366						298	286	333
13	Practice Teach. & Acad.			-021	251								251	160	160
14	General Average								-087						
15	Art			029		225							225	160	160
16	Manual Training			-108		315							315	141	141
17	Gymnasium					326									326
	(City Examination)														
18	History & Principles							-076	-224						-187
19	Methods							-016	160			257			116
20	Total (Exam.)							-001	-045						-034
															176

TABLE VI—*Continued*

Table Number.	Subjects correlated with Practice Teaching	A	C	D	F	H	I	J	X
21	Psychology	386	444				451	240	382
22	Educational Psy.							350	
23	Psy. & Educ. Psy.							370	
24	Hist. & Prin. of Ed.						517	280	
25	"Professional"	388	343	334	189	427	581	342	381
26	Mathematics							063	
27	Science							194	
28	History							364	
29	English							210	
30	Methods	527	395	276	536	346	556	332	416

31	"Professional"	A	571
	correlated with	B	469
	Methods	C	689
		D	436
		E	645
		H	453
		I	721
		J	324

Special for school H

32 Average secondary and average in Training School 278
33 Average secondary and examination (city) 254
34 Average in Training School and examination (city) 443
35 "Professional" in Train. Sch. and examination (city) 408
36 Instruction and Discipline (city marks) 654

2. General View of the Correlations.

In considering the relation between teaching and scholarship in the various subjects, it is seen that the correlation is of a very wide range, from .568 in 3 E, to —.224 in 18 H; but that the general run is low. The average of the averages in column X is .176. This may be more accurately expressed in the following series and the corresponding frequencies. The 92 relationships made with teaching, as given in the tabular view (table VI), may be arranged in 16 groups, each covering .05, as indicated in the series. (These do not include school K, the data for which were secured after these calculations were made.)

Series.	Frequency.	Series.	Frequency.
55	1	15	6
50	2	10	4
45	8	5	2
40	6	0	22
35	8	—5	3
30	7	—10	7
25	8	—15	1
20	6	—20	1

Here the narrow MODE is at .00, *i. e.*, no correlation, while even a larger mode covering half the cases lies between .00 and .337. The average is .18 and the median .175. According to Spearman,[1] a " probable error " of .05 may be admitted in the correlations. Further, if the quotient found by dividing the index of correlation by the ' " probable error " equals 5 or more, it is practically certain that the relation is not one of mere chance. In case the quotient is 5, chance occurrence is only 1 out of 1,249.[2] Now if the upper limit of the mode covering slightly more than half the cases is only .337, and the probable error is about .05, we have not a very favorable condition in the correlations.[3]

The 26 relations made with practice teaching show a higher correlation. Here the range is from .581 to .063, expressed in the following series of 12 groups:

---

[1] *American Journal of Psychology,* xv, 101.

[2] *American Journal of Psychology,* xv, 76.

[3] Several were figured out showing probable error often high, making quotient much less than 5.

Series.	*Frequency.*	*Series.*	*Frequency.*
60	2	30	2
55	2	25	1
50	1	20	3
45	3	15	0
40	3	10	0
35	8	5	1

Here the important mode is .35. The average is .365. The significance of these higher correlations will be considered later.

A few comparisons with other correlations are interesting and suggestive.[1]

	English.	History.	Science.	Algebra.	Drawing.	German.	French.	Latin.
English		62	58	55	15	65	49	62
History...............	62		56	38	10	49	58	43
Science	58	56		40	33	62	48	54
Algebra	55	38	40		20	52	68	54
Drawing.............	15	10	33	20		06	30	01
German	65	49	62	52	06		33	38
French	49	58	48	68	30	33		
Latin	62	43	54	54	01	38		
Av. (without drawing)..	58	51	53	51	16	49	51	50

Here the range is from .65 down to .01, with an average of about .46. Other correlations between various academic subjects, given in Thorndike's *Educational Psychology*, on page 37, are slightly lower than the ones just quoted.

These comparisons are cited here merely to point out more emphatically the low correlation found in the relation between teaching efficiency and the various branches of study and examinations taken in preparation for that work.

[1] A study by Parker of 245 first-year high school students, quoted by Thorndike in his *Educational Psychology*, p. 36.

It may not be surprising to note that in the most favorable case—Teaching and " Professional " in school E—teaching ability and ability in psychology as taught there are identical to the extent shown by a coefficient of .56; but it is certainly surprising that in the history of education, as given in school H, there is a negative correlation to the extent of .224; and perhaps even more surprising that the MODE including about half the number of all the cases lies between no correlation at all and .337.   The significance of these low correlations must be considered later.

We should note also another general aspect of these correlations.   Column X in the tabular view gives the averages of the correlations for the various subjects through the different schools (I and J have no correlation with teaching).   It is obvious that these amounts are greatly reduced by reason of the low correlations of the two schools, C and H, and somewhat modified by the fluctuations in school F. School C is one of the five State Normal Schools (A, B, C, D, E), but school H is a city training school.   It may be well to note the changes in the average correlations when schools H and F are omitted from consideration, for the following reasons :

School H is not of exactly the same class as the others. I need not enter into a careful differentiation between state Normal Schools and city training schools.   No estimate of their relative worth is here implied, but even a slight consideration will show that the students are different—one class coming from the state at large, the other from a much more limited area.   Their previous training and experience probably makes the age of the former class higher than the latter, and age at this period is an important factor.   That the one school is not of the same class as the other is further seen in that the character of the work of the city training school is usually more closely related to the high school work of that city and its work is thus directed to a more narrow field.

The low correlations in this school are perhaps due to the peculiar markings in teaching. For example, in the data for 3 H we find that, out of 154 cases considered, 56, or more than one-third, are put in one class, according to the mark for teaching efficiency. This in itself would not be so bad were the others distributed according to the normal frequency curve. Here is the series: 11, 8, 10, 16, 18, 28, 56, 6, 1. Evidently there is a marked *skew*. The character of these markings will be considered more at length later, but it is evident that the presence of a constant error will allow this school to be set aside from the five Normal Schools.

School F gives records of a very special class of college graduates only. This is sufficient to set it aside for the present.

Omitting schools F and H, we have in column Y the averages for the five State Normal Schools. (The averages are again computed by weighting the individual correlation according to the number of cases considered.) The correlations are now raised in all the subjects, when H and F are omitted, except one, No. 12; and these averages in column Y are possibly better representatives of the true relations.

But the elimination of one other school also may be desirable. It is noted above that the correlations for school C are very low. An examination of the data from this school reveals a peculiar characteristic, which is perhaps the reason for the low correlation. It must be said that it is to be regretted that not more cases were available in this school; yet the peculiar characteristic is so pronounced that it is not probable that a larger number would relieve the situation. Take, for example, number 1 C. Of the 54 cases studied 20, or more than one-third, are in the highest class with respect to teaching efficiency; while on the side of standing in psychology, 27, or just one-half, are in the lowest grade. The following table (VII) taken from the data from school C shows the strange character.

TABLE VII.

Table number	Number of cases	Number in highest grade of teaching efficiency	Number in lowest grade of various subjects
1	54	20	27
2	52	19	9
3	52	19	9
4	54	20	16
5	43	17	12
5-1	46	17	15
6			
6-1	47	17	14
7			
7-1	50	18	4
8	54	20	26
8-1	53	19	7
10	54	20	14
11	54	20	2
12	54	20	6
13	54	20	1
15	51	19	13
16	37	14	3

The striking double skewness here will call for further consideration later; but this is sufficient to make it desirable to consider the average correlations, omitting this school.

The correlation in school D lacks the more constant character seen in schools A, B, and E. The marks given here for teaching efficiency are somewhat peculiar. Yet the error is not so great but that it may for the present be considered with the other three Normal Schools.

If now the correlations in the four schools A, B, D, E, be averaged, as before, we have the correlation of column

Z. (1 D has practically no correlation, but is omitted here by reason of its peculiar character. The correlations for 5-1, 6-1, 7-1, 8-1, are necessarily reduced to the single average of the two schools B and D.) The numbers in column Z stand as the highest correlations we have between efficiency in teaching and scholarship in the various subjects in the Normal Schools.

3. More Specific Considerations with Discussion.

After this general view, we may turn to the consideration of more specific relations. It is not our purpose to consider here all the relations presented in the data, but only a few of the more important.

(1) Teaching and practice teaching.

The tabular view (Table VI) shows the highest correlation to be between efficiency in teaching and practice teaching in the training schools (.443). The averages, as shown in columns X, Y and Z, show practice teaching highest in all cases save three. These exceptions are in column X, where the index is .285. But this is obviously due to the exceptionally low correlation in school H, viz: .025. Omitting this school because of its peculiarities spoken of above, practice teaching heads the list.

Notice further the relations of practice teaching and scholarship in various subjects, as given in 21 to 30. Here, in most cases, the correlation is higher. Note particularly the high correlations between practice teaching and " methods." It would probably be expected that the relation between efficiency in practice teaching and scholarship in various subjects would be closer than that between actual teaching and those subjects; primarily because one pair is within the same institution under similar conditions, while the other, actual teaching, involves much more complicated conditions.

The difference, however, as indicated by the correlations, is significant. It means that the professional studies and special methods in the various subjects in the Normal Schools contribute more directly to teaching under particular conditions than to the broader and more complicated work of the teacher. The higher correlation (.416) for methods and practice teaching compared with that for methods and actual teaching (.327) suggests that these methods are probably made to fit the particular practice teaching, and not the general work required later. 14 and 34 show a much more striking illustration of this same trait. In that case, we have the total work of the school correlating high with the special test in examination (.443), but exceedingly low in the more general and rigid test in actual teaching (—.087). Just so in the Normal Schools. The various subjects of study seem to contribute much to efficiency in practice teaching, but considerably less to actual teaching; but the correlation between practice teaching and actual teaching is again comparatively high. This means that there is an element in the former that contributes directly to the latter.

Compare the correlations of 1 to 20 with those of 21 to 36. It is very clear that the former are lower than the latter. Tables 1 to 20 compare actual teaching with various subjects and examinations. Tables 21 to 36 compare various subjects within the school work. This means that these subjects do not relate to life as they relate to one another. School work is not as closely related to the work the teacher is later called upon to do as it should be. Practice teaching is more closely related to it than are the theoretical studies.

The significance of this is that more practice teaching is needed in the training of teachers. It is also suggested that this practice teaching be as near normal as possible; that is, that it be done under conditions as similar as possible to those of actual teaching. Schools of practice, as such, are liable to be unnatural and abnormal in some particular; and to that extent will be like the various subjects in the curriculum, of comparatively low correlation with actual teaching.

(2) Teaching and " professional " studies.

Next to practice teaching and ranking close to it is psychology (.418). With this should be considered what I have called professional studies: history of education, principles of education, school economy, etc. These, taken with psychology, have a correlation of .336.

An observation of the work in " psychology " given in the Normal Schools shows clearly that this is not the analytic study conducted in colleges and universities. It consists rather in more general studies in human nature. School E shows a high correlation between teaching and psychology (.546). But the avowed aim in that particular work is not introspective analysis, but a broader outlook upon human nature, and especially child nature.

The significance here is the emphasis upon the contribution by those subjects that give breadth of view and general principles. The correlation here is higher than that in particular subjects. The latter give more specific helps; the former, more general enrichment. The data at hand seem to be in support of the position that the student who is preparing for teaching needs to pursue such work as will lead him to recognize and study the larger educational problems, particularly work that will tend to mature him in thought. Most of the 1,185 teachers here considered were probably not more than twenty years of age when these school records were made.   Lack of maturity was probably their greatest handicap in their early teaching.   There can be little doubt, I think, that these professional studies tend to develop a maturity in the prospective teacher which the work in particular subjects does not.

(3) " Methods " and " academic " work.

Normal Schools have been known for their emphasis upon specific methods.   Many Normal School graduates are subjected to grave criticism for their use of cut-and-dried methods.   Much of this criticism is doubtless unwarranted, yet there seems occasion for some such attitude.   The fact of the immaturity of the prospective teacher spoken of in the previous paragraph is probably a reason for this " method " work.   With this there is a common criticism that these same teachers are deficient in a knowledge of subject-matter—that their academic work is weak.   " Too much method work, too little academic work," is a frequent comment.

The question just here is: " What is the relation of their contributions to teaching efficiency in the elementary schools?"   As said in the opening of this chapter, the case is probably different from that among high school teachers.

Taking those schools where marks were obtainable in both methods and academic work, we can arrange these marks for comparison.

Methods	Academic	Difference in favor of Academic
.250	.293	+.043
—.116	—.017	+.099
.010	.049	+.039
.084	.114	+.030
.271	.217	—.054
.120	.140	+.020
.037	.274	+.137
.383	.442	+.059
—.130	.116	+.246
.013	.206	+.193
.473	.381	—.052
.030	—.119	—.149
.135	.151	+.084
.044	—.028	—.072

Thus in the fourteen such cases, ten are in favor of the academic work. The differences are, of course, very slight. The averages shown in column Z (page 71) for 10 and 11 show a slight difference in favor of the method work (the correlations are .327 and .277 for the four Normal Schools only; for all the schools the correlations are .245 and .219). In school H 5 to 11 page 71 are given correlations in the academic work done in the high school. With one exception, that of English (8, no academic), the correlations for the academic work are higher than for the methods. Yet it must be said that the differences either way are not great. In consideration of the stress so often laid upon the need of methods, it is important to note how closely related to this is the academic work in the various subjects.

In view of these facts, there seems less occasion to give instruction in specific methods. _ And it is suggested that the two phases of the work be given about equal attention; or that, if the academic work is made a prerequisite to the work in the training school, most of the time in the latter be given to the professional studies or to more advanced academic work.

Data from school H suggest further need of more academic work, either as a prerequisite or as a part of the regular work. In 34 it is seen that the training-school work prepares for examinations, as indicated by the correlation .443; but 14 indicates that it does not prepare for actual teaching, the correlation being —.087. It is to be noted further that in this same group (33) the academic work in the secondary school does not prepare so well for examinations (the correlation is .254), but that it does prepare even better for teaching (the correlation being .213). It must be said that the marks in teaching for group H are subject to severe criticism, to be pointed out later. For this reason less reliance can be placed upon these figures. So far as they go, however, they would lead us to put more emphasis upon academic work and less on the special methods.

(4) Civil service examinations as a test of the capacity to teach.

Civil service examinations for the purpose of testing the applicant's qualifications for public service have been used in all countries. That examinations serve to stimulate effort to make sufficient preparation, and also to eliminate the unqualified, will be questioned by few. Such examinations are also applied to test the qualifications of teachers in public schools.

The problem here is: " Do the data at hand justify such examinations? Do they test the efficient teachers and eliminate the unqualified?" The only answer at hand is in the correlations between efficiency in teaching and ability in various examinations, in three groups: G, H, and K. Two groups represent graduates of two city institutions preparing students for teaching; the third consists of teachers from three cities in Ohio. The records are 5-2, 6-2, 7-2, 8-2, 18, 19, 20. (See Table VI.)

The correlations in 18, 19, and 20, for schools G and H, are negative, with one exception; and yet so little negative as to be practically zero; *i. e.*, no correlation. If comparison is made with other correlations in school H (3 to 10) it will be seen that these also are practically zero. Thus these city examinations, though limited to the two subjects, history and principles of education and methods of instruction, correspond quite closely to the work in that city training school. With this lack of correlation between the examinations and ability to teach, there would seem to be no justification for such civil service tests. Yet there is certainly about the same justification as for the work of the training school. As will be pointed out soon, the marks for teaching efficiency from schools G and H are such as must be used with care (see page 92).

Referring to the correlations in school K, somewhat different relations are found. Mathematics (which means Arithmetic only), .280, is higher than all other correlations for this subject with two exceptions, and is somewhat higher than the averages as seen in columns X, Y, and Z. Science and history fall considerably below the averages in those subjects, and English compares no more favorably. This means that the work done in history, science, and English in the training schools contributes more to efficiency in teaching than the knowledge of these subjects as tested by the local examinations. And the correlation in mathematics is not so high as to lend much argument in its favor.

Thus the data here used do not afford much justification for examinations as a test for capacity to teach. First, the indices of correlation are in themselves rather low, ranging from .280 to .095, with an average of .196 for school K, while for schools G and H the correlations are distinctly negative. Again, when comparisons are made, correlations are generally lower than for similar work in the training schools. To conclude that the present system of examinations is not an adequate selective agency in providing efficient teachers for our elementary schools, is not warranted because of the original inaccuracies of the data here studied. Yet the facts, so far as they go, seem to point in that direction. Here is the whole problem of the value of set examination to test qualifications. To solve it, data much more complete and accurate are necessary.

(5) Manual arts.

Only two schools, C and E, give measures of ability in the manual arts. These are too meager for much argument. But it is interesting to note how favorably the correlations compare with others in the same school. No argument is needed to show how ability in fine arts, in manual training, including domestic science and domestic art, and in gymnastic work, contributes to efficient teaching in elementary schools. The few facts presented in 15, 16 and 17 support this position.

All the foregoing conclusions are subject to amendment by more accurate data. At the time of the collection of the measures from the 1,185 students the magnitude of the attenuation of correlation produced by chance inaccuracies in the original measures was not recognized by statisticians. In view of Spearman's study of correlation, I should, if I repeated this investigation, take pains to have the teaching efficiency of each person rated by several independent judges, and to obtain, wherever possible, several grades for each person in each trait of scholarship.

In so far, however, as the conclusions drawn here depend upon the relative rather than the absolute magnitudes of the indices of correlation (as most of them do), they would probably be little altered by absolutely accurate original data. I feel confident that the following statements can be made with a high degree of probability.

(1) Ability in teaching and scholarship in professional schools for teachers are related, though not intimately.

(2) Practice teaching is foremost in its contribution to efficiency in teaching and should be carried on in the most normal conditions possible.

(3) Normal School students are doubtless in great need of those studies that tend most to mature them in thought and that suggest the larger educational problems. These are probably those which have been called " professional " studies.

(4) Methods courses do not involve the ability required in teaching to any greater extent than more general professional courses or than academic studies proper.

(5) In so far as we can accept the formally expressed opinions of school principals with respect to teaching efficiency, written examinations are an inadequate means of licensing and promoting teachers, and are less useful than their records in college or training school.

Such an investigation as this could be made with ease and surety if professional schools for teachers gave rational grades in scholarship and kept accurate records of the success in teaching of their graduates. How far the existing records are from this is worth knowing and is the topic of the next section.

(6) Methods of grading.

In this section I shall make some severe criticisms of the methods of grading in vogue in Normal Schools. This does not, however, mean that Normal Schools are specially at fault. High school, college, and perhaps civil service gradings will probably be found upon examination to be equally thoughtless.

One who examines the marks used by individual teachers and principals, the marks in various schools and in different states, is quickly led to the conclusion that there is no uniform measure and seemingly no effort to work together. Each uses his own method, which is supposed to be adapted to a particular purpose determined by the locality and character of the school. But if marks are of any service, they are not simply a record for the individual, but must serve as a communicable measure. And this seems the greatest service. Marks should so measure one's mental trait that they will be intelligible to others, and also serve as a means of comparing different mental traits. To discover such a unit of measure will contribute much to educational work.

The facts concerning grading found in the present study suggest two leading considerations. Many schools and teachers show a distinct tendency to mark high. As pointed out above, marks for efficiency in teaching are given by principals of Normal Schools and by principals and superintendents of schools. The character of these marks can be best seen by noting the form of distribution in various cases, as follows:

1 C.	A	B+	B	B—	C+	C	C—	D
	20	5	7	1	9	7	3	2

1 D.	100,	95,	90,	85,	80,	75,	70,	60,	50,	40,	25.
	16,	14,	27,	1,	4,	6,	2,	1,	4,	1,	4.

1 E.	A	B	C	D	E
	23	41	24	10	3

Thus in school C, we have 54 teachers divided into 8

groups, but 20, or more than one-third, are ranked in the highest class.

In school D, 80 teachers are ranked in 11 groups. One-fifth of these are given a top-most grade of 100, usually regarded as a perfect mark. 57, or more than seven-tenths of the number, are in the three upper grades.

In school E, 101 teachers are divided into five classes. Almost one-fourth are in the first-class; not far from one-half are in the second class. In schools C and D the median line lies between the second and third highest classes; in school E between the first and second.

In school G, using a scale of four divisions, A, B, C, D, 95 teachers are distributed in three classes, A having 2, B having 92, and C having 1. In school H, using the same system as school G, of 150 teachers, 11 are placed in rank A, one in rank C, and the remainder in rank B. In school I the median mark for practice teaching lies between 97.5 and 98 per cent., the range of distribution lying between 99.5 and 78. In this school most of the marks in the various subjects lie above 90, on the old basis of 100 per cent.

Such use of a commonly accepted system of grading tends to destroy the value of that system. This probably means a false estimate of the mental trait in question. Little children are encouraged by a grade of 100 per cent. on a piece of work, and it may be policy to give the grade. But to class one-fifth of a group of teachers in the top rank, marked 100, is doubtless beyond the facts which school men would wish to express. And to class one-half the group in the first one, two, or even three grades when eight or more grades are used is probably not what is wished, if the one who is measuring these mental traits stops to consider what he is doing.

The distribution is often absurdly eccentric.

Thorndike, in the third chapter of his *Educational Psy-*

chology, points out that the distribution of mental traits follows a regular law, except when these traits are influenced by some natural selection. This law is that of the normal frequency curve. Paying no attention to the mathematical accuracy involved, this normal distribution says roughly that at the upper and lower limits of the trait in question there are very few cases: that the number of cases increase, on each side equally, as one approaches the center or median of that trait: that at this point the larger number of cases are to be found. Entirely aside from any technical language this merely means that in the ability to solve algebraic problems among a thousand first-year high school students there will be a large number of mediocre ability: then on each side, for better and for worse, there will be a distribution about equal: that at the two extremes there will be but very few, say two or three of first-class ability, and at the other end of the scale, as many of scarcely any algebraic ability. Such is the normal frequency we have reason to expect when we know of no disturbing agency.

Even a glance at the tables of distribution used in this study shows that they deviate much from the law just mentioned. A few tables will be illustrative.

The first deviation from the law is what I may term bunching: and first, bunching at the extremes. The following distributions are illustrative:

6B: 1, 4, 2, 3, 2, 3, 1, 4, 3, 7, 6, 7, 5, 6, 9, 9, 6, 17.
5C: 17, 3, 6, 1, 7, 5, 2, 2.
4C: 3, 1, 1, 5, 1, 9, 2, 1, 1, 5, 1, 1, 5, 1, 1, 16.
13D: 18, 14, 30, 1, 5, 5, 2, 1, 5, 1, 5.
7E: 25, 6, 10, 30, 8, 1, 11, 3.

Here are three cases where the bunching is at the upper extreme, and two cases where the large group is at the lower extreme. Both cases are improbable, unnatural, and quite likely not really desired by the one giving the marks.

Another case of bunching is at intervals in the distributions. For example:

 5A: 1, 4, 1, 5, 2, 20, 2, 7, 10, 4, 23, 4, 8, 14, 3, 21, 6, 3, 2, 8, 2.
 7B: 1, 1, 2, 1, 1, 3, 1, 7, 1, 1, 1, 9, 1, 1, 6.
 4C: 3, 1, 1, 5, 1, 9, 2, 1, 1, 5, 1, 1, 5, 1, 1, 16.
 8-1D: 16, 9, 31, 12, 18.
 7E: 25, 6, 10, 30, 8, 1, 11, 3.

Here the bunching is probably due to the tendency to use more frequently certain marks than others. 80, 85, and 90 are more readily used than 83, 87, 91. In 5A, the greater frequencies are seen to be at intervals of five. Likewise, A, B, C, are more readily given then A—, B+, C+.

Both these cases of bunching are in all probability due to carelessness or indifference in grading, rather than the presence of some selective agency. The presence of a selective agency would disturb the normal frequency, and one might then expect a regular grouping, due to the disturbing cause. This, then, means that the marks given are not precise measurements of the trait in question: but are rather mere excuses for the desired grading.

A second case of the distribution not being normal is that which is so conspicuous in schools G and H. Here the distribution lies between A and C, though with the use of the scale A, B, C, D, but with almost all the cases in B. This necessitated an arbitrary further distribution into ten grades, as seen in all the tables for schools H and G. Even with the attempted improvement, the number of cases under B is too large to allow any suggestion of a normal distribution. The very fact that the marks found were almost wholly of grade B is plain evidence that little or no discrimination was used in giving these grades. It was only with much patient search that even a score of C grade teachers could be found among many hundred, and only two or three of D grade.

This evident lack of discrimination calls in question the use of marks at all. Marks are intended to be measures of mental traits. Measurement implies the presence of differences. Now classing individuals in large groups in the methods just pointed out means a lack of discrimination,— or it may be a fear to express one's own convictions. In either case, or in any case, such use of marks is destructive to the whole system. They lose their significance. Men must soon cease to have any confidence in them as measures: for they do not measure.

The study of these marks leads to certain suggestions or recommendations as to the nature of grading individuals, of measuring their mental traits.

(1) Grading should be by relative position. It is impossible to use the present system as an absolute measure. One can not say that the individual stands 100 per cent. in history, 90 per cent, or 83½ per cent. An individual mental trait is too intangible and too variable to be submitted to that kind of measurement. Strength can be measured by the pound-weight: swiftness of foot, by the distance per minute, but scholarship in mathematics or history is really to be measured by its relative position in a group with which it can be compared. We might, for example, referring to the series of marks below, say of these 147 teachers: " Six of them stand in the fore-front, without making a discrimination among these six. There are ten others so near alike that we may give them second rank compared with

Grade	95	90	85	80	75	70	65	60	50	40
Frequency	6	10	31	24	31	28	8	5	3	1

the best six. In the succeeding lower ranks are the groups 31, 24, 31, 28, 8, 5, 3, 1. In this case the six set the standard of measurement, by which others stand or fall." Or we might begin at the lower extreme and take the single man in this case as the standard, and measure all the others *upward*. But the best man or the poorest man does not serve well as the standard for comparison. This should rather be the *central tendency of the group*. This should serve as the standard, and the better and worse be measured by their deviations from the central tendency. Thus we measure individuals in a group by their deviations from the central tendency in respect to a particular trait. This is far preferable to an imagined absolute measure. The per cent method of grading and the letter method, if properly used, are really measures by relative position. John should be marked 80, not because that number expresses his degree of mentality, but because he is slightly above the larger portion of the class, the average of which is rather arbitrarily placed at, say 75. In this way we are measuring the individuals of a group in terms of a function of that group.

(2) The range of distribution should be comparatively wide. In schools G and H, the distribution is in three groups, though on a scale of four. Yet in these two schools, there is practically no distribution: that is, almost all cases are put into one group, B. Here is an extreme case of almost non-discrimination. One step removed from this extreme is that of two groups. These two may stand for the satisfactory and the unsatisfactory groups. And this is a very practical division. A principal or superintendent may, for his immediately practical purposes, divide his teachers into the satisfactory and the unsatisfactory classes. The one, he retains; the other, he dismisses. The eighth grade teacher, at the close of the year, may divide her fifty pupils into two groups; forty are satisfactory and are passed into the high school: the ten are unsatisfactory and are retained. This is the mere act of accepting and re-

jecting. There are times when a carpenter may direct that a pile of lumber may be divided into two classes: that which is two or more inches in thickness, and that which is less. The former he can use; the latter is not wanted. But his various labors soon ask for finer measures and there are many practical purposes to be accomplished through a closer discrimination. A merchant asks the principal of a school for his two most capable boys in figuring. The one most capable in the class is valedictorian; the next most capable presents the salutation in the closing exercises of the school: there are prizes and honors (and dishonors) to be distributed according to the standing of the individuals in class. These are practical purposes to be met by a closer discrimination between the mental traits of the pupils of the school.

There is also a new demand for this finer measurement of mentality. Students of education in their study of problems pertaining to school work are in need of these facts. The problem of educational values, *e. g.*, does the study of Latin enable the pupil to accomplish more in algebra, can not be answered by knowing whether or not the student "passed." A closer discrimination of his algebraic ability is necessary. All inquiry as to the relation between mental traits calls for the finer measures of mentality. The old 100 per cent basis implies a possible grouping into 100 divisions. Yet probably such a range is never used. In the data here used, the range is from 100 to 15, yet there are few cases where twenty divisions are used. The number of divisions must depend much upon the number of individuals graded, and much upon the motive in the grading. Where greater discrimination is wanted, the number of divisions must be greater. Where acceptable or non-acceptable is all that is wanted, two classes are sufficient. Further, where the number of individuals is small, the number of groups will be small.   In school D, scholarship in the various subjects is marked by the three measures 1, 2, 3.   In the tables for this school, these three grades are expanded into five by the method of averages used, and even this means little discrimination where a hundred or more individuals are involved.

The range of distribution should be sufficiently wide that one may be able to locate at least the extreme 10 per cent: that is, it would be well to be able to speak definitely of the best 10 per cent and of the poorest.   In the use of only three divisions, this would necessitate 80 per cent in the middle class.   Here is too little discrimination.   It would be well to be able to speak of half the class grouped about the median grade.   Retaining our 10 per cent extremes, this would call for at least five groups, viz.: 10, 15, 50, 15 and 10 per cents.   But to throw half of the whole number into one group is to measure very roughly that group, and it is also desirable that the extremes be less than 10 per cent: for one would wish to know the one, two, or three most capable boys in a school of 50 pupils.   It would seem then that at least seven or nine divisions should be used, in case of even as few as twenty individuals.   More than fifteen or eighteen grades become cumbersome and call for closer discrimination than is probably needed.

The 100 per cent method of marking, so commonly used, is usually assumed to be an absolute measure—a certain per cent of perfection being the measure.   Difficulties here are evident.   Foremost of all is the fact that no work ever *really* merits a perfect mark.

(3) The normal curve of distribution should serve as the standard.   This normal course, as pointed out earlier, means simply—that, under normal conditions, of the members of a large group a considerable portion will be nearly equal in a given trait, and will represent the central tendency of

the group. Above and below, for better and for worse, other members are about equally distributed: at the two extremes are to be found only comparatively few, representing the very best and the very poorest. Psychology D, table VII, is not at all normal: and is probably not a just rating. It is probably not true that the great majority are at the very top.

In actual application, the teacher would need first to decide upon the number of groups to make, according to the suggestion made above. Then pick out those of mediocre ability for the median class. The others are to be distributed above and below. In using this method, one must be careful not to follow it too rigidly. A perfectly normal distribution is probably not possible. 3, 5, 12, 20, 38, 20, 12, 5, 3 is expected to be somewhat altered. Yet this is a type to which all groups doubtless do tend.

This method seeks the natural course, in two particulars: (1) Mental ability is really judged by no absolute standard, but by relation to the same kind of ability in other individuals. (2) Most of such abilities are neither very good nor very bad, but have what is known as the normal curve of distribution.

That the suggestions made above concern a real issue is abundantly proven by the following table (Table VII) which gives some 60 samples taken at random of the grades used in the present study. The scales for these grades are given at the left of the table.

TABLE VII

SAMPLES OF GRADES GIVEN IN NORMAL SCHOOLS

	Psychology A.	Psychology B.	Psychology C.	Teaching B.	Hist. of Ed. B.	Education B.	Teaching C.	Hist. of Ed. F.	Pract. Teach. A.	Pract. Teach. F.	Pract. Teach. H.	Mathematics A.	Mathematics B.	Science H.	History A.
100															
99					5										
98			1		6							1			2
97															2
96															2
95		1	4		14	2	5	6				4	3		10
94			1	1		2				1		1	2		1
93		2		4	1	3	1	1					2		
92		5	7	7	5	6	1		1			5	1		8
91		1		1	3	3			3	2		2			1
90		4	13	13	38	7	9	6	2	3		20	5		24
89	1	2		2		6			4	2		2	1		1
88		14		15	6	19	2		6	3		7	5		5
87		5		10		6	3	1	5			10			
86		2		8	3	9			5	2		4	1		4
85	4	11	4	5	13	10	4	4	18	7		23	7	1	16
84		13		3	2	5		2	7			4	3	6	3
83	11	5		5	1	6	3		9	3		8	1	6	
82	2	7		6	5	6	5		11	4		14	5	7	9
81		2				4			5	2	1	3		7	
80	12	6	3	7	17	7	4	4	25	5	10	21	12	10	19
79	5		1	3		1			4		21		7	15	3
78	13	4		5	1	1	2	1	19	3	29	6	12	20	9
77	16	3		2			1	1	6	3	25	3	4	24	1
76	9	6			6		3		4	1	30	2	5	25	7
75	53	4	27		7		9	2	15	1	36	8	18	20	3
74	6									1	2			5	
73	7				2						1			7	
72	1				1					1				1	
71										1					
70	5				1				2			2		1	1
69															
68					1										
67															
66															
65	1														
64															
63															
62															
61															
60					1										
15	1														
N	147	97	54	97	144	103	52	28	151	45	155	150	92	155	131

TABLE VII—*Continued*

	Teaching C.	Teaching E.	Science E.	Methods E.	Man. Train. E.	Education E.	Mathematics E.	Science E.	History E.	Psychology E.	Teaching C.	Prac. Teach. J.	Psychology J.	Ed. Psycho. J.	Teaching G.	History of Ed. E.
A	20	23	18	12	39	19	16	18	25	19	14	7	10	9	8	19
A—			30	16			27	30	6	21						21
B+	5		24	23		5	11	24	10	25	4					23
B	7	41	18	31	35	6	13	18	30	18	7	32	18	24	41	19
B—	1		7	7		1	12	7	8	9	1					6
C+	9		2	8		9	12	2	1	4	6					1
C	7	24		4	22	7	8		11	5	3	11	20	19	13	12
C—	3		3			3	1	3	3		1					1
D+																
D	2	10			1	2					1	1	4	5	2	
D—																
E+																
E		3										2	1		3	
N	54	101	102	101	97	52	100	102	94	101	37	53	53	57	67	102

	Psy. & Ed. Psy. J.	Hist. & Prin. J.	Professional G.	Mathematics J.	Science J.	History J.	English J.	Methods J.
A	7	1	1		2	3	4	7
A–B	9	3	8	2	3	1	1	4
B	13	31	28	2	11	8	12	29
B–C	10	9	10	1	3	3	9	25
C	16	10	15	9	21	24	21	39
C–D	6	2	2		4	3	7	16
D	3	5	2	3	4	4	6	13
D–E		1	1	3		3		
E				4	1	1		7
N	64	62	67	24	49	50	60	140

TABLE VII—*Continued*

	Teaching A.	Psychology D.	Teaching D.	History K.	Teaching F.	Teaching D.	Methods K.	Mathematics H.	Prac. Teach. D.	Mathematics K.
100		16	11	2		15	11		19	21
95	6	14	10	17	3	14	22	5	14	13
90	10	27	24	32	3	32	19	12	31	30
85	31	1		10	6	1	13	16	1	3
80	24	4	4	18	4	4	12	16	4	14
75	31	6	5	7	8	6	2	22	6	4
70	28	2	1	9	7	2	5	10	2	7
65	8			2	2		2	27		4
60	5	1		5	3	1	1	10	1	2
55				1				11		
50	3	4	5	2	6	5		12	5	1
45				1						1
40	1	1				1				2
35										
30										
25		4	4			5			6	2
15										1
N	147	80	64	106	42	86	87	150	89	106

	Teaching D.	Education D.	Mathematics D.	Teaching K.	Mathematics D.	Science D.	History D.	English D.	Methods D.	Professional D.
1	21	17	21	14	21	14	10	16	9	19
2	5	4	5	21	4	23	8	9	19	13
3	29	28	29	44	38	-27	23	31	31	12
4	15	5	15	16	11	14	5	12	21	8
5	13	11	13	11	14	5	18	18	4	7
N	83	65	83	106	88	83	64	86	84	59

I regret that it is impossible for me to print here in full the original data from each of the 1185 teachers' records, and their correlation tables showing the detailed facts for each of the 140 coefficients calculated. To do so would require some hundred pages of tables. I append a few sample tables which give the details in the case of some of the important relationships.

In the nine tables that follow the scale of grading for teaching is given at the left of each table; that for the subject correlated with teaching, at the top. The figures in the body of the table show the distribution of all the individuals studied and, by their position, indicate the standing for each individual in the two subjects compared. At the right and bottom are the sums of the several arrays. It should be said that in the first two tables (schools H and G) the scale at the left was originally A, B, C, D, though only A, B, C, was actually used. 1 corresponds to A; 2-7 to B; 8-10 to C. Thus in the first table 11 teachers are graded A; 136, B; and 7, C. The B and C grades were scattered by taking into account the + and — marks upon some of the grades.

TABLE VIII (1)

SCHOOL H

Teaching and City Examination (Average)

	90	89	88	87	86	85	84	83	82	81	80	79	78	77	76	75	74	73	72	71	70	62	59	58	56	
1									1				1	1	1			1		1	4		1			11
2									1	1	2					1				1	2					8
3											1	2	2				1	1	1	1	2					10
4					1				1	2	2		2			4	1				4					17
5			1					2	1	1	1			2	1	3		1	1		4					18
6				1			5			1	1	3	1	1	4	1	1	1	1	2	7					29
7	1	1				1	3	2	6	2	3	3	3	2	3		3	3	2	3	9	1	1	1	1	54
8							1							1	1	1		1	1		1					6
9																										
10																							1			1
	1	1	1	1	1	1	9	4	10	7	9	8	9	7	10	10	6	6	6	8	33	1	3	1	1	154

TABLE VIII (2)

SCHOOL G

Teaching and City Examination in " Methods "

	56	54	53	52	51	50	49	48	47	46	45	44	43	42	41	40	39	38	37	36	35	34	
1										1				1									2
2																							
3										1				1									2
4								1		1	2	3	1	1		1	1	1					12
5						2	1	1		2	2	2	1	2				2			1		16
6										2		4	1	1					1		1		10
7		1	1	1	1	2	3	2	3	2	6	5	1	4	5		3	3	1	1	4	1	50
8									1		1												2
9																							
10																			1				1
	1	1	1	1	2	5	4	5	4	4	10	9	7	9	1	4	6	2	2	4	2	1	95

TABLE VIII (3)

SCHOOLS A, B, C AND E

Teaching and Psychology

	1	2	3	4	5	
1	10	11	7			28
2	16	21	4	3		44
3	12	30	13	7	1	63
4	21	42	77	17	5	162
5	2	5	18	11	4	40
6		4	7	2	5	18
7	10	11	8	11	4	44
	71	124	134	51	19	399

TABLE VIII (4)

SCHOOLS A, B, C, D AND E

Teaching and " Professional"

	1	2	3	4	5	
1	17	14	4	4	1	40
2	20	20	14	4		58
3	24	47	27	14	6	118
4	12	40	38	14	8	112
5	10	20	30	11	5	76
6	5	7	11	7	7	37
7	3	4	9	8	1	25
	91	152	133	62	28	466

TABLE VIII (5)

SCHOOL A

Teaching and Methods in English

	95	90	85	80	75	70	65	60	50	40	
94		1									1
93			1								1
92		1	1								2
90	2	3	3	3	7		1				14
89					1						1
88			5	3	1				1		10
87			1	1	2						4
86			2								2
85	1	4	10	6	1	8		1	1		32
84			1	2	1				1		5
83			1	2	2	2	1	1			9
82	1		1	1		2					5
80	2	2	4	4	7	6	2	2			29
79						1					1
78			1	1	1	1	2				6
77						1	1				2
76						1					1
75			3		7	3	2	1			16
73				1							1
70			2			1				1	4
68						1					1.
67						1					1
55									1		1
	6	11	36	24	30	28	9	5	4	1	154

TABLE VIII (6)

SCHOOL B

Teaching and Methods in English

	94	93	92	91	90	89	88	87	86	85	84	83	82	81	80	79	78	77	
96							1												1
95	1								1										2
92							1												1
90	1	1						1											3
89							1		1										2
88				1	1			1					1		1				5
87			1		1														2
86							1					1							2
85			1		2		1	1		1		1							7
84										1									1
83		1	1		1														3
82					1										1		1		3
81					1		1	1			1					1			5
80		1	3		1	1	1	1	2	1		1	1		1				14
79			1		1		1	1		1									5
78			1		1		5	1	1		1			1	1				12
77					1			1			1				1	1	2		7
76					1		1		3	1			1		1	1	1		10
75								1	1			1	2		2	1		2	10
	2	3	8	1	12	1	14	9	9	5	3	4	6	1	8	3	4	2	95

TABLE VIII (7)

SCHOOL C

Teaching and Methods in English

	A	B+	B	B—	C+	C	C—	D	
95	1		1		2	1			5
90	7	1			1			1	10
89					1				1
85	2				1	1	1		5
80	2		1		2	1			6
79						1			1
75	8	4	5	1	2	3	2	1	26
	20	5	7	1	9	7	3	2	54

TABLE VIII (8)

SCHOOL D

Teaching and Methods in English

	1	1-2	2	2-3	3	
100	1	1	11	1		14
95	4	2	4	2	2	14
90	3	6	9	4	7	29
85			1	1		2
80	1			1	1	3
75	2	1	1		2	6
70	2					2
60		1				1
50		2		1	2	5
40				1		1
25	1			2	2	5
	14	13	26	12	17	82

TABLE VIII (9)

SCHOOL E

Teaching and Methods in English

	A	B	C	D	E	
A	10	6	4	1		21
AB	5	9	5			19
B	3	20	7	3		33
BC	1	5	6	3	2	17
C		1	2	3	1	7
	19	41	24	10	3	97

NOTE.—Criticism has been made upon this study to this effect: To establish a correlation between scholarship in psychology and ability to teach, for example, does not show that the study of psychology contributes to efficiency in teaching, but only that that study serves as an effective means of selecting those who have qualities required in successful teaching. An answer to this may be found in the quotation from Pearson given on page 61. But in either case the practical consequences are the same.

CHAPTER V

GENERAL TRAINING OF ELEMENTARY TEACHERS

INTRODUCTION

1. *The Problem.*

There is in New York and Massachusetts an increasing attention paid to the training of elementary teachers. New Normal Schools have been erected within the last few years and the efficiency in equipment has been much extended. Attendance upon these schools has increased to meet the demand. The larger cities have their own Normal Schools. Training classes in various local high schools are much encouraged. While the graduates of these training schools are in much demand,[1] there is a demand in some localities for teachers who are " self-made," *i. e.*, teachers who, in profiting by experience, have gained success. There are also a few college graduates teaching in the grades. We may well ask from what kind of training do the most efficient teachers come. The individual and personal element must, of course, enter largely, but in the present inquiry we shall set that aside.

2. *Generalizations.*

This is too limited a study to insure completely valid results. The generalizations indicated are as follows:

1. There is a slight tendency to promote the more efficient teachers into the upper grades.

2. Amount of experience seems to have little influence on the degree of teaching efficiency.

3. There is no indication that the amount of secondary school training has any relation to teaching efficiency.

4. Only 3½ per cent of the teachers studied are college

---

[1] Yonkers, N. Y., has few teachers who are not Normal School graduates.

graduates. These, as well as those who attended college but did not graduate, have a rank below the average in the schools in which they are teaching.

5. Normal School graduates do not stand emphatically above the average teacher. It is clear, however, that graduates of city training schools, and those who have not studied in pedagogical schools are somewhat inferior to the average teacher.

METHOD

1. *Data Collected.*

For this inquiry answers were secured to the following questions :

1. In what grade are you teaching?
2. How many years have you taught?
3. How many years did you study in the high school?
4. How many years did you spend in college?
    Did you graduate?
    Give the name of the college.
5. Professional work.
    What school did you attend?
    How many years?
    Did you finish the course?

These questions were sent to elementary schools in New York and Massachusetts, containing from 8 to 31 teachers. These teachers answered the questions, after which the principal of the school expressed his estimate of the general teaching efficiency of each teacher by grouping them according to their relative rank. For example, one principal grouped his 27 teachers as follows :

	First rank.	Second rank.	Third rank.	Fourth rank.
Number of Teachers ...	5	8	10	4

The data here used come from 33 schools and represent 507 teachers. With but few exceptions, each teacher answered all the questions, so that the data are complete, so far as they go.

2. *Regrouping.*

The ranking of the teachers of the 33 schools differed much in the number of groups into which the corps of teachers was divided. For example, one principal divided his teachers into a first, second and third rank. Others made 5, 8, 12, and even 22 groups. In this last group were 22 teachers, who were thus arranged in perfect serial order from the most efficient teacher to the least efficient teacher. To use all these together they must be reduced to the same number of groups. The following table (IX) shows how they were reduced to five groups. Here the principle used was that the extremes should be disturbed as little as possible. Thus, in an original grouping into 10 we now have: first rank remains first rank; second and third become second rank; the fourth to the seventh become third rank; eighth and ninth become fourth rank; and the tenth becomes fifth rank.

TABLE IX

TABLE OF REGROUPING.

Original Groups	First Rank	Second Rank	Third Rank	Fourth Rank	Fifth Rank
5	1	2	3	4	5
6	1	2	3-4	5	6
7	1	2	3-5	6	7
8	1	2	3-6	7	8
9	1	2-3	4-6	7-8	9
10	1	2-3	4-7	8-9	10
11	1	2-3	4-8	9-10	11
12	1	2-4	5-8	9-11	12
13	1	2-4	5-9	10-12	13
14	1	2-4	5-10	11-13	14
15	1	2-5	6-10	11-14	15
18	1	2-6	7-12	13-17	18
19	1	2-6	7-13	14-18	19
20	1	2-6	7-14	15-19	20
22	1-2	3-7	8-15	16-20	21-22

DISCUSSION.

1. *First question.*

Any inquiry as to in what grade the better teachers are found has really no direct bearing on the question of efficiency in teaching. Consideration is given to it here only for the purpose of locating the cases studied in the questions following.

The desire for promotion is natural in teaching as in other occupations. Just what promotion in the elementary schools means is perhaps somewhat questionable. There is a feeling among such teachers that an advance to a higher grade in the school is given in recognition of greater efficiency, is promotion. In some schools teachers in the higher grades are recognized as the stronger teachers and are paid accordingly.

For the present purpose I have rearranged the groupings of the various schools into three groups by the method suggested above. The following is the table of distribution, the first grade including a few designated as kindergarten teachers:

TABLE X

Grades	1	2	3	4	5	6	7	8	9	
1	44	23	17	12	17	15	15	22	8	173
2	45	16	23	27	20	18	19	12	3	183
3	32	11	19	15	11	13	5	6		112
	121	50	59	54	48	46	39	40	11	468

"As a rule, the best-trained teachers, those receiving the highest salaries, should be placed in the lower primary and the upper grammar grades, while the young and inexperienced should be placed in the intermediate."[1] This seems like a very plausible theory and there is a little evidence of

[1] J. H. Phillips, Superintendent, Birmingham, Ala. Quoted in the *Report of the Chicago School Commission for 1900*, p. 52.

its practice here. Table X shows the lower and upper grades to have a little better representation in the first rank, while the third to seventh grades have more of the second rank teachers.

2. *Second question.*

What do our data indicate as to the relation of experience to relative standing in teaching efficiency? We have such questions as these: Does the teacher's standing increase with her experience, *i. e.*, do the older teachers stand foremost, or is there a certain amount of experience at which a teacher is in her " prime of life?"

In this study I have divided the thirty-three schools into two divisions: In the first division I have rearranged into five groups all schools already in five or more groups; in the other I have arranged into three groups those schools already in three or four groups. In the former group are 387 cases; in the latter, 117 cases—making 504 cases considered. The number of years' experience in teaching is given in nine groups, as follows: 0, 1, 2, 3, 4, 5, 6 to 10, 11 to 15, 16 and over. The following table gives the distribution. The numbers at the top give the number of years' experience; those at the left indicate the rank of the teachers; the others show the individual cases in each.

TABLE XI(1)

TEACHING EFFICIENCY IN RELATION TO EXPERIENCE

Amount of Experience

Rank	16+	15—11	10—6	5	4	3	2	1	0	Total
1	9	16	18	2	2	1	2			50
2	16	16	28	10	6	4	7	4		91
3	16	14	51	10	12	13	10	12	1	139
4	14	15	18	6	3	6	5	10		77
5	5	7	10		1	2	1	4		30
Total	60	68	125	28	24	26	25	30	1	387

When turned into percentages the entries in the above table give the following:

TABLE XI(2)

Amount of Experience

Rank	16+	15—11	10—6	5	4	3	2	1	0	Total
1	15	23.6	14.4	7	8.3	3.8	8			13
2	26.7	23.6	22.4	35.8	25	15.4	28	13.3		23.5
3	26.7	20.6	40.8	35.8	50	50	40	40	100	36
4	23.3	22	14.4	21.4	12.5	23.1	20	33.3		20
5	8.3	10.2	8		4.2	7.7	4	13.3		7.5

That is, 15 per cent of those who taught sixteen years or more are in the first rank; 13.3 per cent of those with one year's experience are in the lowest rank.

The true standing in each group may be well seen from the median of each group; that is, the point which marks the dividing line between the better half and the poorer half in each group of teachers. These medians are calculated upon the series of five groups according to teaching efficiency. I omit the single case with 0 years' experience.

16+	11—15	6—10	5	4	3	2	1	Totals
2.81	2.63	2.82	2.70	2.83	3.11	2.85	3.40	2.88

A treatment of the other 117 cases in three groups gives practically the same results. The following is the table of distribution:

TABLE XII

Amount of Experience

Rank	16+	11—15	6—10	5	4	3	2	1	0	Totals
1	8	9	11	4	3	2	1			38
2	6	10	19	2	2	4	2	4	5	54
3	3	3	9		1	1	1	6	1	25
Totals	17	22	39	6	6	7	4	10	6	117

The medians on the basis of a series of three are as follows:

Experience	16+	11–15	6—10	5	4	3	2	1	0	Totals
Median Rank	1.58	1.70	1.95	1.25	1.50	1.87	2	2.66	2.10	1.88

Fig. 1.

From Table XI.

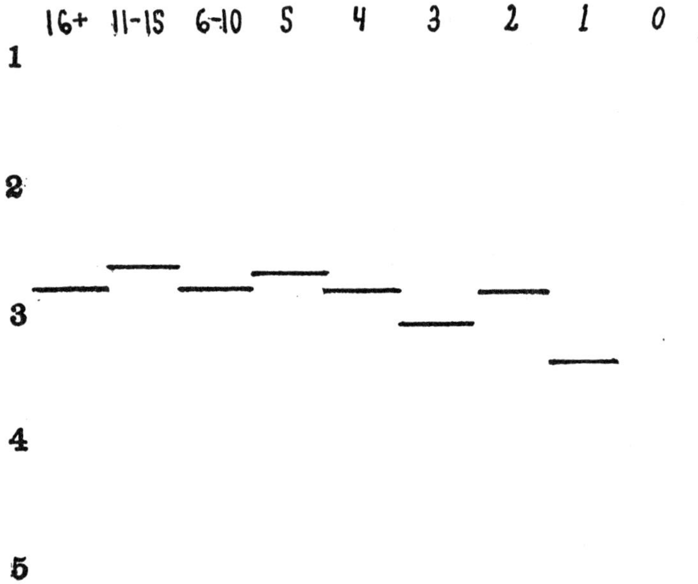

From Table XII.

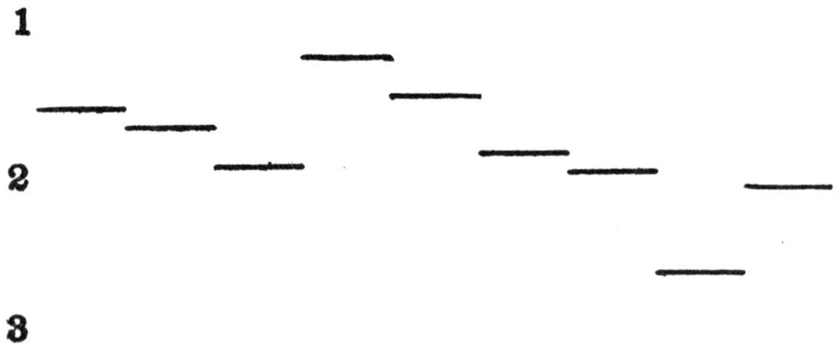

Figure 1 presents graphically the comparison of amount of experience with efficiency in teaching. The numbers at the left are the rank in teaching efficiency.

The Pearson formula for the index of correlation for the 387 cases with the better grading gives .097. This would be much smaller but for the group with one year of experience. Apart from that group there is practically a zero correlation. It must be said, then, in answer to the relation between experience and teaching efficiency that beyond the first year of experience it is practically *nil*. After the first year the amount of experience is not an important criterion for efficient teaching in the elementary schools. The importance of this fact, if it is confirmed by later researches, to administrators of school systems is obvious.

3. *Third question.*

Here the question is: Is there evidence of any difference in the teaching efficiency of those who took more or less than the usual four years in high school work. That is, does a post-graduate year in the high school tend to strengthen the teachers, and will less than four years in the high school give a lower teaching efficiency? There were 429 answers to this question. Of these 12 were ambiguous in that 7, 9, 10, 12, etc., were the answers. These twelve persons evidently misunderstood the question or used " secondary schools " in a sense not intended. One answered, " Don't know." Discarding these 13 replies we have 416 to be considered.

Only 19 report having taken an extra year in the high school; 169 spent less than four years in the high school. Any significance in more or less than four years of high school work must be found, if at all, in the distribution of these 19 and 169 in the schools in which they are ranked. This, for the evident reason that the other 288 took the full course, and the question here is consequently as to the more and less. If the former are found among the better of each group, there is evidence that the extra year contributes directly to teaching efficiency; if the latter are found among the lower of each group, there is the same evidence. For the line of demarcation between the better and the worse, I have taken the median of all the cases in each school. The significance of having spent more or less than four years in high school work depends, in the second place, upon the amount of deviation from this median. That is, if the 19 who spent more than the usual four years were found in the first rank when the median is, for example, 4.5, the contribution of this extra year is greater than if these 19 were in the third rank. The results are as follows: Of the 19 who did extra work in the secondary schools, 9 stand above the median, 10 below. The sums of the deviations from the medians are 12.60 above and 24.46 below. Of the 169 who spent less than four years, 85 are found above the median, 84 are below. The sums of the deviations are 197.33 and 225.93 respectively.

Thus, so far as these results go, there is no proof that the amount of time spent in secondary school work has a beneficial influence on teaching efficiency, and the evidence is that it has little or none. It may be said that with but few exceptions these 19 and 169 have done other work than the high school in preparing for teaching. There is evidence that many of the 169 took their secondary studies in the Normal Schools with their professional work.

4. *Fourth question.*

In many parts of the country a college training is required for high school teachers. The tendency in all school systems is in this direction. In contrast to this, there are only a few college graduates in the elementary schools.

The opinion has been expressed that the time is soon coming when these teachers also must be college graduates. On the other hand, it is strongly asserted that this more advanced study tends to suppress that sympathy with child nature so much needed in the elementary schools. The data at hand are rather meager, but they tend to support the latter position.

Of the 517 teachers replying, only 19 are college graduates. There are 14 others who have been in college from one to three years. Of the former group, the following are the colleges and the amounts of deviation of each teacher from the median rank in each group (+ indicates above the median; —, below):

Boston University		— 8.50
College of the City of New York	+ .83	
College of the City of New York	+ .83	
College of the City of New York		— .17
Manhattan		— .17
Mt. Holyoke		— .25
New York University	+ .83	
Normal College of the City of New York.		— 2.50
Pennsylvania College	+ 5.	
Radcliffe	+ 2.50	
Smith	+ .45	
Smith		— .80
Smith		— 4.25
Smith	+ 3.75	
Syracuse		— 1.50
Tufts	+ .20	
Wellesley		— .25
Wesleyan		— 9.50
Woman's College of Baltimore		— 1.
Total	+ 14.39	— 28.89

Thus, of the 19 college graduates, 11 rank below the median; only 8 above. And the deviations on the lower side are considerably greater than on the upper: 28.89 and 14.39 respectively. Of the 14 who attended college but did not graduate, 10 are ranked below the median and only 4 above, while the sums of the deviations are —26.30 and + 7.39 respectively.

In this consideration four things are to be noted:

1. The small proportion of college-bred teachers in the elementary schools. Of those studied, only 3½ per cent are college graduates and slightly less than 3 per cent have studied in college without graduating.

2. The relative standing of these in teaching efficiency. Both classes rank below the average teacher.

3. The relation between the two groups. The college graduate stands higher as an elementary teacher than does the one who merely tasted college and did not take a full course.

4. The possibility that only the less gifted college students enter elementary teaching.

5. *Fifth question.*

Here the inquiry is as to the contribution to efficiency in teaching made by professional study. The method used here is to count the number of Normal School graduates who stand above and below the median rank in each of the 33 schools. That is, is the number of teachers who are Normal School graduates above the median greater than the number below? But we must also take into account the amount above or below which each teacher is. We must give more credit to a teacher who stands first in a group of twelve than to one who stands fourth rank where the median is 5.50.

The whole number of Normal School graduates here considered is 290. Of these, 158, or 53 per cent, are above the medians of the several groups. Below are 132, or 47 per cent. This means that so far as numbers go Normal School graduates as teachers are but slightly superior to the average. Considering the amounts of deviation in each of the 290 cases, we find that the total amount of deviation above the medians is 303.25, while that below is 341.22.

In this group there are 90 teachers who are graduates of city training schools. Thirty-three, or 37 per cent, are above the median; 57, or 63 per cent, are below. Here is considerable difference on the basis of number. The sums of the deviations are: above, 115.45; below, 132.51. Thus, the argument of the numbers is supported and we can conclude that the city training school graduate is below the Normal School graduate.

There are 69 teachers in this group who have had no pedagogical training. Thirty, or 43 per cent, are above the median, while 39, or 57 per cent, are below. This argument against the teacher with no pedagogical training is further supported when the deviations are considered. These are: above, 88.80; below, 141.04.

The conclusion, then, is that the Normal School graduate is not much above the median standard, but that both those who had their preparation in city training schools and those who have had no pedagogical training at all are distinctly, though not far, below the standard. The importance of such a result is well worth considering by students of education.

CHAPTER VI

THE INSTRUCTORS IN THE NEW YORK STATE NORMAL SCHOOLS

Interest in the study of education and attention to the training of teachers is on the increase. Normal Schools, city training schools, teachers' colleges, and schools of education in universities are much more prominent than a few years ago, and there is indication that increased attention to this work will continue for some time. Aside from the research work in educational problems conducted in educational departments of universities, these institutions and the Normal and training schools emphasize the need of training teachers for their work in elementary, secondary, and even higher schools. Educational literature abounds in emphasis upon the need of training teachers. Discussions in educational gatherings bear upon these same subjects. On the other hand, there seems to be little said or written on the subject of this chapter: Are the instructors in the Normal Schools adequately prepared for their work? It is, indeed, well to emphasize the training of those who are to teach in our public and private schools, or even in our colleges and universities; but what of those who are teaching these prospective teachers?

There are at present no established criteria for successful, efficient teaching. Perhaps none can be discovered. If teachers are born, not made; if teaching is wholly an art, not at all a science; if there are really no grounds for a scientific inquiry as to what elements are needed as a preparation for teaching, we have no occasion to point out to the prospective teacher certain prescribed principles for instruction. There are at least elements commonly accepted as essential. First, scholarship, to some degree beyond that of the student under instruction. There is a strong tendency—and in some places even a decision—to require that teachers in our high schools shall be college graduates. This same principle, so characteristic in the German school system, is to be emphasized more and more throughout our educational system: viz., the teacher must be more in advance of the student under his instruction. A second belief is that some study of educational problems and some training in the art of teaching are essential. In evidence of this, note the large number of teachers in New York state who have had pedagogical training. The following is a classification of the teachers of the state according to the kind of licenses held: [1]

Pedagogical Training,	Normal School	3979
	Training School	3323
Examination,	State	328
	College	197
	Commissioners	9143
	Temporary	436

This means that considerably more than one-third of all teachers in the state have had pedagogical training. In Massachusetts the increase in the number of pedagogically-trained teachers has been marked in the past decade.[2]

Finally, there is much reliance upon personality and individuality as essential in successful teaching. This is more easily recognized than analyzed and developed.

The first of these principles seems especially applicable to

[1] *Report of the State Superintendent*, 1902, pp. 10-11.
[2] *Report of the Board of Education*, 1902, p. 104.

the teaching staff in a school for teachers—emphatically so in the Normal Schools. As was said, little attention has been paid to the qualifications of these instructors. The only reference to this particular matter which I have as yet found is by Atkinson.[1] He finds the preparation of the teacher in secondary schools in this country inadequate, in that the Normal School in which he receives his training really supplies no more knowledge than he is supposed to teach. He notes in this connection the few college graduates on the faculties of certain of these Normal Schools, adding: " The presupposition may be advanced that those who are not college graduates or their equal in scholarship will not understand how to make the most of what the college graduate brings." I think it may be safely asserted, further, that a Normal School instructor who has not had the experience and uplift of collegiate work, is not sufficiently ahead of his students, many or all of whom are high school graduates, to have a high and permanent influence upon them.

The design of the Normal Schools of New York, as stated in most of their catalogues, is " to furnish trained teachers for the public schools of the state." [2] Thus, while the Normal Schools may aim primarily to prepare teachers for the elementary schools, they do also pretend to prepare for secondary work as well. The " Normal College " at Albany states its purpose as that of " giving instruction in the science and art of teaching," [3] and here there is a distinct intention to prepare teachers for the secondary schools. Further, all of these schools recognize college graduates

---

[1] *Professional Preparation of the Secondary Teacher in the United States*, p. 24.

[2] *Circular*, New Paltz, 1902-3, page 3.

[3] *Circular*, 1901, page 3.

and invite them to their work. Albany provides special classes for such. Thus there is really in mind work of a higher grade. This should call for attention to the qualifications of the teachers in such schools. But even if the work were wholly for elementary teaching, is it not right to presume that these prospective teachers may look for highly educated teachers in their instruction? Degrees are not an assurance of educated men. Yet, in general, they do indicate intellectual standing and educational equipment. In this chapter degrees will be used as a partial measurement of the equipment of teachers. The treatment of this theme aims to show:

1. The degrees held by the instructors in the Normal Schools of the state of New York, their distribution and relations; that there are too few of collegiate standing, and rather too many of higher degrees without collegiate standing; that the schools do not compare favorably with other pedagogical institutions.

2. The institutions by which these degrees were granted; that many of the collegiate degrees are from institutions of not high standing, while the higher degrees are too much limited to the home state, and are too often honorary.

3. The preparation of those instructors who are without degrees; that too many are without adequate training, having only that offered by the school in which they are now teaching.

4. Similar details of one school throughout its history; that the conditions here are very similar to those of the state at large, showing that the latter—on this basis—has made little change or progress.

5. That consequently there are too few of the higher trained men and women engaged in the training of our elementary teachers; that the inspiration given by graduate study is wanting; that too few of these teachers have

studied at the centers of greatest advance in educational work.

6. Similar facts concerning 49 representative State Normal Schools throughout the country; that these show conditions similar to those found in the New York schools, and thus substantiate the conclusions drawn.

The rather large number of tables used will speak strongly for themselves. They say more than can be written about them. They will be their own argument, and will suggest a few conclusions.

The data used for the study of the New York schools come through officials at Albany, and are to be relied upon. They are not to be found, as yet, in any printed documents. These data consist of lists of the faculties of each of the twelve Normal Schools in the state. With the name of each instructor are given the several degrees he holds and the names of the institutions from which such degrees were received. Eight of the twelve schools give also the schools at which those who have no degrees have received diplomas, or have studied.

Table XIII shows in detail the degrees held. Roman numerals designate individual schools. The Arabic numerals in the first column indicate the whole number of instructors in each of the schools. The Arabic numerals in the second column stand for the individual instructors who hold degrees. The marks in the various columns at the right (of these first two) tell the degrees held by each individual. A summary is given for each school, and in table XIV is given a summary for all the schools.

For example: School I has 24 instructors, 13 of whom hold degrees of some kind. Instructor number 10 holds four degrees, viz.: Pd. B., Pd. M., A. B., Ph. D. The total degrees held by this school are: Ph. B., 7; Pd. M., 3; A. B., 7; A. M., 8; Pd. D., 6; LL. B., 1; LL. D., 2.

TABLE XIII

DEGREES OF NORMAL SCHOOL INSTRUCTORS

		Pd.B.	Pd.M.	Pd.D.	B.L.	Ph.B.	B.S.	A.B.	S.M.	A.M.	Sc.D.	Ph.D.	M.D.	LL.B.	LL.D.	M.P.
I																
	1							I		I		I			I	
	2									I		I				
	3									I		I				
	4									I						
	5									I					I	
	6													I		
	7	I						I				I				
	8	I								I						
	9	I	I					I		I						
	10	I	I					I				I				
	11	I						I		I						
	12	I	I					I				I				
	13	I						I								
24	13	7	3					7		8		6		I	2	
II																
	1			I		I										
	2									I						
	3							I								
	4									I						
	5									I						
	6						I									
	7							I		I						
	8									I						
	9				I											
	10							I								
	11							I								
	12									I						
22	12			I	I	I	I	4		6						
III																
	1							I		I		I				
	2						I									
	3								I							I
	4															
	5							I								
	6							I								
	7				I											
	8			I				I								
	9												I			
	10	I														
29	10	I		I	I		I	4	I	I		I	I			I

TABLE XIII—*Continued*

	No.	Pd. B.	Pd. M.	Pd. D.	B. L.	Ph. B.	B. S.	A. B.	S. M.	A. M.	Sc. D.	Ph. D.	M. D.	LL. B.	LL. D.
IV	1									1		1			
	2							1							
	3							1							
	4							1		1					
	5							1		1					
	6							1							
	7					1									
24	7					1		5		3		1			
V	1							1		1		1			
	2					1									
	3							1		1					
	4							1							
	5						1								
	6						1								
	7							1							
	8												1		
25	8					1	2	4		2		1	1		
VI	1									1		1			
	2											1			
	3									1		1			
	4											1			
	5							1							
	6							1							
	7	1						1							
22	7	1						3		2		4			
VII	1									1		1			
	2									1		1			
	3						1			1		1			
	4			1											
	5					1									
	6							1							
	7	1						1							
	8							1							
	9						1								
17	9	1		1		1	2	3		3		3			

TABLE XIII—*Continued*

		Pd. B.	Pd. M.	Pd. D.	B. L.	Ph. B.	B. S.	A. B.	S. M.	A. M.	Sc. D.	Ph. D.	M. D.	LL. B.	LL. D.	B. D.
VIII																
	1							I		I						
	2									I						
	3							I		I						I
	4							I								
	5							I								
	6							I		I						
	7	I														
	8											I				
20	8	I						5		4		I				I
IX																O. M.
	1							I		I	I					
	2						I									
	3					I										
	4							I		I						
	5							I	I							
	6							I				I				
	7															I
	8							I								
	9															I
	10				I											
	11							I								
22	11				I	I	I	6	I	2	I	I				2
X																
	1			I						I						
	2					I										
	3			I												
	4											I				
	5							I				I				
	6									I						
	7									I						I
20	7			2		I	I			3		2				I
XI																
	1									I						
	2					I		I		I	I					
	3							I		I		I				
	4							I								
	5	I				I										
23	5	I				2		3		3	I	I				

TABLE XIII—*Concluded*

		Pd. B.	Pd. M.	Pd. D.	B. L.	Ph. B.	B. S.	A. B.	S. M.	A. M.	Sc. D.	Ph. D.	M. D.	LL. B.	LL. D.	B. D.	O. M.	M. P.
XII																		
	1							I		I		I						
	2					I												
	3							I		I								
	4							I		I								
	5									I								
	6					I												
	7							I										
	8							I										
	9					I												
	10						I											
	11						I		I									
	12							I		I								
	13							I		I								
13	13					3	2	7	1	6		1						
261	110	12	3	5	3	10	10	52	3	43	2	22	2	1	2	1	3	1

TABLE XIV

THE NUMBER OF INSTRUCTORS

A. In each Normal School faculty.
B. Holding degrees of college standing.
C. Holding higher degrees (without B).
D. Holding pedagogical degrees (alone).
E. Holding special degrees (alone).
F. Holding no degrees.

	A	B	C	D	E	F
I	24	7	5	1	1	11 (one man is in C and D)
II	22	7	5			10
III	29	6	1	1	2	19
IV	24	6	1			17
V	25	7			1	17
VI	22	3	4		1	15 (one man is in C and E)
VII	17	6	2	1		8
VIII	20	5	2	1		12
IX	22	9			2	11
X	20	2	4	2	1	13 { (one man is in C and D) (one man is in C and E)
XI	23	4	1			18
XII	13	12	1			0
	261	74	26	6	8	151 (four counted twice)

Total degrees for the twelve State Normal Schools are:

Pd.B........ 12	A.B........ 52	LL. B...... 1
Pd. M....... 3	S.M........ 3	LL.D...... 2
Pd.D........ 5	A. M....... 43	B.D........ 1
B.L. 3	Sc.D....... 2	O.M. 3
Ph.B........ 10	Ph.D....... 22	M.P. 1
B.S. 10	M.D. 2	

Our real problem centers about the number of instructors holding degrees of collegiate standing; this for the reason that pedagogical degrees are as yet of inferior rank, and many higher degrees are obtained in special ways and do not always indicate even the rank of a collegiate degree; while special degrees are what their name implies. We cannot, therefore, consider the 110 out of the 261 instructors as all acceptable degree men. If this discrimination seems unjust, it must nevertheless be accepted for the purposes of this study and allowance made if the conclusions reached here are not admitted. A classification of these degrees is given below. It is to be distinctively understood that this chapter does not claim that the 26 instructors with higher degrees have no degrees of collegiate standing. Undoubtedly some of them have; on the other hand, it is known that some of them have not. The data asked called for all degrees, and in general this request seems to have been complied with. There is no other way than to treat the data as given, and be willing to make some allowance if later information requires it.

(1) Degrees of college standing: B. L., Ph. B., B. S., A. B.

(2) Pedagogical degrees: Pd. B., Pd. M., Pd. D.

(3) Higher degrees: S. M., A. M., Ph. D., Sc. D.

(4) Special degrees: M. D., LL. B., LL. D., B. D., O. M.

(5) Higher degrees without collegiate degree: There is some indefiniteness as to this item. In some of these cases, I know, the higher degree is without the preliminary college degree; in others there is an uncertainty.

It is evidently unjust to the 74 of collegiate standing to say nothing more of them. Further credit must be given those who have, in addition to their collegiate work, attained to higher and special degrees. Further, it is well to know to what extent those of higher degrees—without collegiate standing—have also pedagogical or special degrees. All of this is shown in Fig. 2, which gives a complete distribution of all the 261 instructors in the Normal Schools on the basis of the number and kind of degrees, and the absence of any degree at all.

Some of the results as shown in Fig. 3 are quite surprising. Only 28 per cent—a little more than one in four—of all Normal School instructors are college graduates. Does this argue that the Normal Schools, standing as the trainers of the teachers of the public schools of the state, maintain that a college education is a minor matter in the shaping of popular education, that inspiration and efficiency are better gained from those without this higher intellectual training. Ten per cent of the instructors have advanced beyond the collegiate standing. This, it must be said, speaks well; the more so, if these schools stood for elementary training only. Yet we can not but encourage an increase of this class. The low per cent of pedagogical degrees is perhaps surprising. It is probably complimentary, considering the present standing of this degree and the requirements for its attainment. The 10 per cent of higher degrees without college standing should probably be in part distributed among the 28 and 10 per cent above, as explained earlier. The 58 per cent having no degrees at all seem an emphatic indication of the low equipment of these teachers. Nearly three out of every four of all Normal School teachers have not even the pedagogical degree, to say nothing of collegiate or higher training. What preparation these teachers really have will be pointed out later. (See Table XVI, page 133).

It is interesting to compare briefly the instructors in University departments of education with those in Normal Schools with respect to academic attainments. Choosing certain typical university schools of education and including in the comparison the numerous teachers in the practice-schools and in technical departments who come under the general heading of officers of instruction, we obtain the following comparison:

A, whole corps of instructors.
B, degrees of college standing.
C, higher degrees, in addition to those of college standing.
D, higher degrees, without college standing.
E, no degrees.

	A	B	C	D	E
Normal Schools	261	74	29	26	151
Schools of Education	159	83	49	?	70
In percents of A.					
Normal Schools	100	28	11	10	58 (4 spec. & ped.) }[1]
Schools of Education	100	53	31	?	44 (4 spec.) }

If we should collate the academic career of the individuals in university Schools of Education whose work parallels that of the staff of a New York ' State Normal School,' the proportion of collegiate and post-collegiate degrees would increase.

[1] No account is here taken of those holding special and pedagogical degrees.

FIG. 2.

DIAGRAM ILLUSTRATING DEGREES OF COLLEGE STANDING AND THEIR RELA-
TIONS TO OTHER DEGREES.

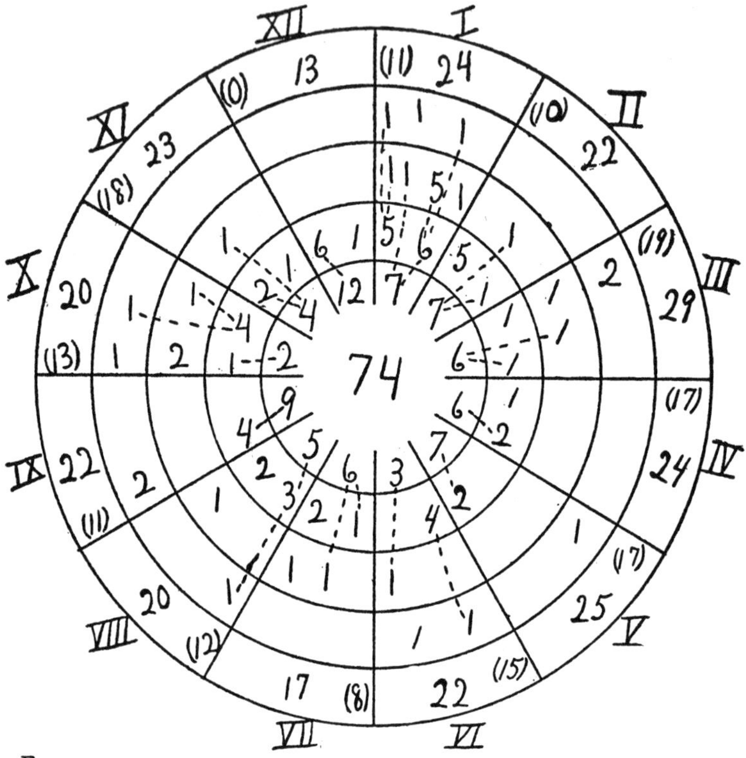

EXPLANATION:

1. Roman numerals at margin indicate the school.
2. The center, 74, gives the total of college degrees.
3. The inner circle gives the college degrees of each school.
4. The second circle gives the higher degrees of each school.
5. The third circle gives the pedagogical degrees of each school.
6. The fourth circle gives the special degrees of each school.

Dotted lines show the relation. For example, in School I there are 7 instructors with degrees of college standing. Of these 7, 6 have higher degrees. Of these 6, 5 have pedagogical degrees, and 1 has a special degree. There are 5 with higher degrees (without college degrees). Of these 5, 1 has pedagogical and 1 a special degree.

7. The fifth circle gives the total number on the faculty. In parenthesis, those without any degree.

FIG. 3.

SUMMARY OF THE FACTS OF FIG. 2.[1]

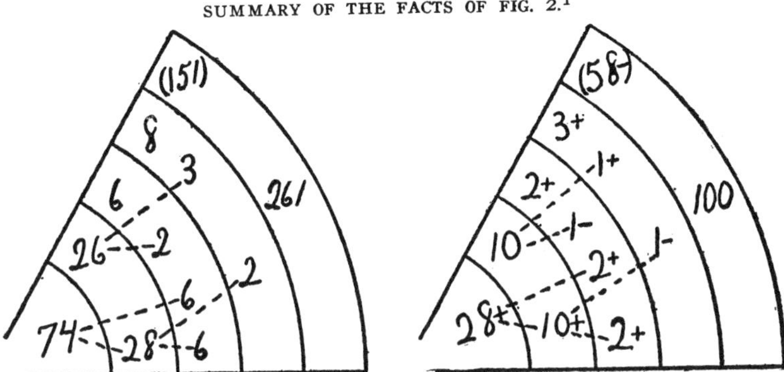

1. Total degrees of college standing, 74, or 28% of the faculties.
Of these 74, with higher degrees are 29, or 11% of the faculties.
Of these 28, with pedagogical degrees are 5, or 2% of the faculties.
Of these 28, with special degrees are 2, or 1% of the faculties.
Of these 74, with pedagogical degrees (only) are 6, or 2% of the faculties.

2. Total higher degrees, without college standing, 26, or 10% of the faculties.
Of these 26, with pedagogical degrees are 2, or 1% of the faculties.
Of these 26, with special degrees are 3, or 1% of the faculties.

3. Total pedagogical degrees, without college standing, 6, or 2% of the faculties.

4. Total special degrees, without college standing, 8 or 3% of the faculties.

5. Total with no degrees at all 151, or 58% of the faculties.

We may next note briefly the colleges and universities represented by the collegiate and higher degrees already considered. These institutions are put into two classes as indicated in Table XV, page 130. It may be mentioned in this connection that most of the few pedagogical degrees are from the Normal College at Albany. The Michigan Normal College and Wisconsin University are also represented. The sources of the few special degrees need not concern us.

This table (XV) gives all the colleges and universities

[1] See *Errata*, p. 152, for corrections.

represented in the Normal Schools, together with the number of times each is represented, both by collegiate and higher degrees. In the former, Wellesley leads, followed closely by Cornell, Harvard, Smith, Vassar, Yale. In the latter, Syracuse leads, closely followed by Rochester, Cornell, Illinois Wesleyan.

TABLE XV

COLLEGES AND UNIVERSITIES FROM WHICH DEGREES HAVE BEEN TAKEN BY INSTRUCTORS IN THE NEW YORK STATE NORMAL SCHOOLS

Collegiate		*Higher*	
Wellesley	8	Syracuse	6
Cornell	7	Rochester	5
Harvard	5	Cornell	4
Smith	5	Illinois Wesleyan Univ	4
Vassar	5	Columbia	3
Yale	5	Hamilton	3
Columbia	4	Harvard	3
Syracuse	4	Amherst	2
Rochester	3	Bucknell	2
Chicago	2	Colgate	2
Illinois Wesleyan Univ	2	Lafayette	2
Michigan	2	Michigan	2
Oberlin	2	Yale	2
Dartmouth	1	McKendree	1
Wisconsin	1	Trinity	1
Queens	1	Radcliffe	1
Westminster	1	Alfred Univ.	1
Scio	1	Westminster	1
Colorado	1	Univ. of State of New York.	1
Wabash	1	Nat. Nor. Univ. (O.)	1
Alma	1	Johns Hopkins	1
Elmira	1	Rutgers	1
Rutgers	1	St. Lawrence	1
Colgate	1	Illinois State Nor. Univ.	1
Boston Univ.	1	Oberlin	1
St. Lawrence	1	Union	1
Amherst	1	Hobart	1
Adrian	1	Genesee	1
Hobart	1	Smith	1
Genesee	1	Wellesley	1
Middletown	1	Berlin	1
Michigan Nor. Col.	1	France	1
Bucknell	1	Jena	1
		Leipsic	1
		Strassburg	1
		Zurich	1

Concerning table XV, three things are to be noted:

1. Columbia University and Cornell University are not as well represented as might be expected.

2. On the collegiate side, institutions outside of the state are well represented among the leading schools and number about two-thirds of all. On the side of the higher degree, New York has one-half of all represented. No state is so large and well equipped but that the introduction of men from other states will be advantageous. In this respect the representation seems good.

3. Some of the higher degrees are not especially significant of advanced work and seem out of place in a list with degrees from Cornell, Columbia, Harvard, Johns Hopkins and Berlin.

Two institutions must have special reference. It is seen in Table XV that five of the Normal School instructors have higher degrees from Rochester University. Four of these degrees are Doctor of Philosophy. But the Ph. D. from Rochester does not stand for advanced study. That university does not give this degree for work done,[1] but only as an honorary degree. These degrees cannot, then, be justly ranked with the others.

The second institution for special reference is Illinois Wesleyan University. Three of the four higher degrees are Ph. D., and one is A. M. The standard of the degrees may be estimated when one reads in a recent catalog: "The Graduate Degrees of A. M., and Ph. D. are conferred only for work, the nature and extent of which will be stated on inquiry."[2] It is well known that this work may be done wholly in absentia. "The university does not give instruction in these courses, nor does it lay down a pre-

---

[1] Private letter from the President.

[2] *Catalogue* for 1903, page 12.

scribed order of yearly or semi-yearly study. . . . . The latest editions of the texts will be used in the preparation of examination papers. . . . Ph. D. matriculates are required to present themselves at the university for the last examination." [1]

A similar list of the sources of the degrees of instructors in university 'Schools of Education' shows to the decided advantage of the latter, especially in the case of the higher degrees.

The third part of this study concerns itself briefly with the preparation of those teachers who have no degrees. Of the 261 Normal School teachers there are 151 of this class. But data available permit a consideration of only 89 of these, representing eight out of the twelve schools. It can scarcely be doubted that these eight schools are fairly representative of all.

Table XVI, page 133, explains itself. But special attention is called to the statement of percentages which follows it. Two of the statements may be repeated here.

1. Fifty-eight per cent of those having no degree are educated in the school in which they teach. That is,

2. Thirty per cent of all Normal School instructors have had no further educational preparation than that offered by the school in which they are at present engaged as teachers (the elementary and perhaps high school study is, of course, not considered here).

These two statements mean that over one-half of those with no degree—which usually means very little educational training—and nearly one third of all teachers in Normal Schools are turned right back as teachers where shortly before they were students. This practice is in violation of the

[1] *Announcement—Graduate and Non-Resident Department*, 1904, pp. 8-10.

principle advocated at the opening of this chapter and approaches the Lancastrian system of monitorial instruction. The pernicious effects of such a practice will be referred to later.

TABLE XVI

THE PREPARATION (AS FAR AS IT IS KNOWN) OF THE 151 INSTRUCTORS IN THE NEW YORK STATE NORMAL SCHOOLS WHO HAVE NO DEGREES.

A, the number in each school with no degree.
B, graduates of the school in which they are teaching.
C, graduates of other Normal Schools of the State.
D, those who have studied in various schools.[1]

	A	B	C	D	
I	11	8	2		No data for one.
II	10	5	2	3	
III	19				No data.
IV	17				No data.
V	17	9	4	4	
VI	15	8	3	4	
VII	8				No data.
VIII	12	6	3	2	One is of high school only.
IX	11	3	4	4	
X	13	12		1	
XI	18				No data.
XII	0				
	151	51	18	18	

It is safe to consider the eight schools for which data are given as typical of all the twelve schools. Upon this basis, we have 89 teachers without degrees, distributed as in the table above.

Thus it may be said of teachers without degrees:

[1] These are Pratt Institute, 4; Emerson School of Oratory, 2; Harvard Summer School, 2; Art League (N. Y.), 1; Elocution in Philadelphia, 1; Yale Physical Training, 1; Cooper Union, 1; Academie Francaise des Etats Unis, 1; Gorham Normal School, 1; Framingham Normal School, 1; Mansfield Normal School, 1.

58 per cent. are graduates of the school in which they teach.
20 per cent. are graduates of other Normal Schools of the state.
20 per cent. have done some work in the various schools, named above.
1 per cent. is a high school student only.
1 per cent. is unaccounted for.

A similar study of instructors in university ' Schools of Education ' who lack degrees, shows a much smaller proportion of students trained only by a single institution, much less ' in-breeding,' and much more study abroad.

In line with the foregoing, a study was made of the professional preparation of the faculty of one school from its foundation in 1869 to 1894.[1] The history of the school published at that time gives a brief account of each person who had been upon the faculty in those twenty-five years. This account seems to speak as highly as possible of those instructors, such as, " He has been highly honored with the degrees A. B., A. M., D. D., LL.D." The account can therefore be relied upon as giving all the degrees held by the 78 men and women who, in the period of 25 years, held positions in the school.

The summary of results is as follows:

```
Total number of instructors............. 78
Holding collegiate degrees.............. 20
Holding higher degrees ................. 20 (5 of these Ph. D.)
Holding special degrees ................  4
Holding no degrees.....................  46
```

If we consider the Ph. B. as a degree of college standing in this particular case although it comes from a correspondence school, we have 20, or slightly more than one-fourth of the instructors in the school, who have completed work of college standing. So also there are 20 holding higher degrees, A. M. and Ph. D. There are 4 who hold special

---

[1] *First Quarto-Centennial History*, Potsdam Normal School.

degrees. Thirty are Normal School graduates, 17 of whom are graduates of this school. There are 16 who have done no higher study at all. Putting these with the Normal School graduates, we have 46 out of the 78 who have no degrees.

We may now make comparison with the state at large as seen in Fig. 3, page 129.

	State.	*This School.*
Holding college degrees	28%	26%
With higher degrees	11%	17%
Holding only higher degrees	10%	4%
Holding no degrees	58%	59%

If the past record of this school is typical of the others of the state, there is little difference between the present and past. This would mean that the Normal Schools are making little headway in securing instructors of more advanced educational qualification.

The institutions which granted degrees to the instructors of the school under consideration are the following,—the numbers at the left indicate the number of degrees granted:

College Degrees.	*Higher Degrees.*
3 Rochester.	3 Rochester.
3 Syracuse.	3 Syracuse.
2 Union.	2 Hamilton.
2 Yale.	1 Boston University.
1 Amherst.	1 Bowdoin.
1 Bowdoin.	1 Colgate.
1 Cornell.	1 St. Lawrence.
1 Hamilton.	1 Union.
1 Howard.	1 University of New York.
1 Illinois Wesleyan.	1 Yale.
1 Michigan.	
1 Packee Collegiate Institute.	
1 Williams.	

It must be remarked that four of the five Ph. D. degrees

given are honorary degrees; given by four of the universities in this list. Such practice speaks for itself, and a record of four such degrees out of five " speaks louder than words."

By way of a brief summary of the leading points of this study, the following statements may be made.

I. As to degrees:

1. Twenty-eight per cent of all instructors in the Normal Schools have had college training. (This may be slightly increased owing to lack of definiteness of data).

2. Eleven per cent of all instructors attained higher degrees in addition to collegiate standing.

3. Normal Schools have only one-half the proportion of college-trained instructors found in one University School of Education, and only one-fourth the proportion of those who have advanced to higher degrees. They compare but slightly more favorably with other university Schools of Education.

II. As to institutions represented:

A wide range of institutions are represented by the collegiate degrees, but the higher degrees are much more limited to the state. Yet neither list as a whole shows the strongest institutions and some are questionable.

III. As to the non-degree teachers:

1. Fifty-eight per cent of all Normal School instructors have no degree.

2. Thirty per cent of all Normal School instructors

have received no higher education than that of the school in which they are teaching.

3. The non-degree teachers show very little educational training outside of the Normal School work.

The foregoing considerations afford material for much discussion, but a few conclusions only will be made. This whole study may seem to be in criticism of the *status quo* of the teaching staff of the New York State Normal Schools. Circumstances seem to warrant just this. Yet some will say that the Normal Schools are doing a good work, commensurate with the needs and proportionate to that of other institutions. As said above, we have not at hand criteria for measurement of the efficiency of this work. The whole argument is upon the assumption that the work done in the Normal Schools is not what may properly be expected—or at least wished—at this time. The effort of this chapter has been to point out one of the vital elements of weakness and in so doing suggest a remedy.

One other assumption has been evident: viz., that the college degree stands for much in the way of educational equipment: the college degree has here been used as a measure of efficiency. To this many, Normal School men especially, may object: and it is admitted that many men with college degrees are most conspicuously unfit for educational work. In spite of this the college man as such stands as a type of man educationally qualified when compared with men lacking this training.

A third consideration was referred to earlier: The Normal Schools undoubtedly stand primarily for the training of elementary teachers. Yet the truth is, they do attempt to prepare some teachers for secondary schools. In either case, if our second assumption is valid, and if we have regard for the German principle mentioned above, the Normal School student, as a prospective teacher, may well expect and demand that the larger portion of his instruction be at the hands of teachers of at least collegiate training.

Conclusions may be stated as follows:

1. There are too few college-trained men and women on the teaching staff of the Normal Schools of New York. More such teachers are needed to give a more scholarly character to the work in place of the more narrow and shallow work in " methods." Such a class of teachers is further needed to bring a broader and deeper experience and insight into the work and life of the Normal School. Thirdly, there is need of this class of teachers that the Normal Schools may be brought into closer touch with colleges and universities. The estrangement is now too great. The Normal School needs the influence of the universities that are doing the advanced and more progressive work in educational problems.[1] The Normal Schools lag behind, satisfied with the work done in the past. Finally, this higher class of teachers is needed to attract a better class of students to these schools. The common report is too true that young people attend these schools who are able to do nothing else. A stronger corps of teachers will attract a stronger class of students.

2. The Normal Schools are fairly represented by teachers who have degrees in advance of the collegiate standing. This higher attainment is not to be insisted upon for all or even for the many, yet it should be encouraged. Normal Schools should be doing some research work in the way of actual tests of practical school work. Such work calls for the student trained in graduate study.

3. It is probable that it would be advantageous if more

---

[1] See a study by Meriam, in *American Education*, 7: 97-99, 1903.

of the leading institutions were represented in the Normal Schools. Too few of the degree men in the Normal Schools come from the centers of greatest advance and most progressive methods in educational work.

4. The proportion of teachers who have had no more advanced training than afforded in the Normal Schools themselves should be much lessened. Without this improvement there is too much of the Lancastrian monitorial system, the instructor only a lesson in advance of his students. The effect of such work is too evident to need comment. But there is in this connection a greater evil. Our inquiry has shown that 30 per cent of all Normal School instructors have received no educational training in advance of the school in which they are now teaching. The 30 per cent, too, includes only those who are without degrees of any kind. The percent would be somewhat increased if the degree men were added. The pernicious effect of this in-breeding (to use a strong but characteristic expression) is evident; the more injurious, indeed, the more lacking these teachers are in a broad educational training. This practice narrows, stultifies, and makes barren the work and life of the school thus guilty.

To supplement the study of degrees held by Normal School faculties of New York state, I have taken 49 other schools scattered throughout the country. This study is based upon the catalogs of these schools in the years 1901 and 1902. Not all catalogs show the preparation of the various instructors. Out of a nearly complete file of the catalogs of State Normal Schools, 49 supply the information sought. It must be admitted that this material is not as reliable as that of the New York schools: yet it is probable that any generalizations made will be not far from the truth. In this list janitors, engineers, nurses, gardeners, etc.

are not counted, though in a large number of the schools they are listed with the " faculty."

Table XVII, pages 142-144 gives in detail the facts collected from these catalogs. For convenience, I have divided the states into four groups, viz.: The North Eastern, The North Central, The Western, and The Southern. States not represented are those having no state Normal Schools, or not giving desired information in the catalogs.

The number in the column marked ' Professional department' indicates the instructors in that department. The next column shows the number in the ' Training department.' In only a few schools, however, is this differentiation made. The numbers in the various degree columns indicate the number of instructors in that particular school holding such degrees, e. g., in school 12 (of 1), 7 hold the degree M. E.; 4, the A. B.; 4, the A. M.; 3, the Ph. D.; and there are three with special degrees. The little figures 1, 2, 3, etc., refer to the following key:

1. Instructor also holds A. M. degree.
2. Instructor also holds M. S. degree.
3. Instructor also holds A. B. degree.
4. Instructor also holds B. S. degree.
5. Instructor also holds Ph. B. and B. L. degrees.
6. Instructor also holds Pedagogical Degree.
7. Instructor also holds Special Degree.

For example, in school 12, 2 of the 3 holding the Ph. D. degree also hold the A. M. degree.

These 49 schools may be taken as typical of the Normal Schools throughout the country. The question asked here is the same as that asked concerning the schools of New York state, viz.: What is the preparation of the instructors in these schools, judged by the degrees they hold? It must again be emphasized that the mere possession of a degree is no absolute criterion of efficiency in teaching. But the tendency of all educational institutions is to demand of their instructors the possession of collegiate or higher degree, as evidence of having pursued courses that prepare for educational work. The degree, then, serves as *one* mark of preparation. In these 49 Normal Schools scattered throughout the country outside of New York state, we find a total of 1063 teachers. 188 of these belong to the training departments. In some of these schools, this means teachers in the grades. We shall, therefore, exclude these from consideration. It may be noted, in passing, that 9 of these hold collegiate degrees: 3 have the A. M. degree; 3, the A. B. degree; 2, the B. S. degree; and 1, the Ph. D.

Omitting these 188, we have 875 Normal School teachers to consider. The character of the data forbids going into detail as in the consideration of the New York teachers. For example: in only a few cases can we tell what lower degree is held by one who has an A. M. or a Ph. D. Such a case, however, may be seen in group III, school 3, in column headed Ph. D. Here are two men holding this degree, one of whom holds the A. M. (marked 1) : the other, a special degree (marked 7). We shall, therefore, consider only the total.

TABLE XVII

NORTHEASTERN STATES

State	School	Professional Dept.	Training Dept.	Pd.B.	Pd.M.	Pd.D.	M.E.	B.L.	Ph.B.	B.S.	A.B.	S.M.	A.M.	Ph.D.	Special.
I — Massachusetts.	1	16	13							1	1		1	1	
	2	13	19										1		
	3	8	18								1		2		
	4	16	9							1	2			1	
	5	15									1		1[3]	1[1][3]	
Ct.	6	7	19												1 M.D.
Maine.	7	10											1		1 M.D.
	8	10								1					1 LL.D.
R.I. N.J.	9	10	12					1		1			1	1	
	10	33	31						1	2 / 2	2 / 3		2 / 1	4	1 M.D.
	11	22	12								2	1	2		
Pennsylvania.	12	29					7				4		4[5]	3[1][1]	1 M.B., 1 M.D., 1 B.O.
	13	24					7						4[3]	1[1]	2 B.O., 1 B.E.
	14	29					2				6	3	3[4]	1	1 D.D.
	15	26					10				2		9[6]	1[1]	
	16	44		2	1		7				3[6][6]	3	3	5[1][1]	
	17	19					5				1		3	3[3][6]	
	18	30					7					2	7	3[1][1]	1 M.D., 1 M.B.
Vermont.	19	5											2		
	20	5											1		
	21	6											1		
Total.	21	377	133	2	1		45	1	1	6 / 2	25 / 3	9	48 / 1	25 / 1	12 special.

TABLE XVII—*Continued*

WEST CENTRAL STATES

II

State	School	Professional Dept.	Training Dept.	Pd.B.	Pd.M.	Pd.D.	M.E	B.L.	Ph.B.	B.S.	A.B.	S.M.	A.M.	Ph.D.	Special.
Ill.	1	17	11					1		1	2		5	2[1]	
Ia.	2	50		3	2			1	7	2	1	3	14	2	1 U.S.A., 1 Ph.M.
Kan.	3*	37						1		1			4	4	2 B.M., 1 Ph.M., 2 B.P.
Mich.	4	20	9	2	1					2	3	1	2 1		
Mich.	5	55	14					3	6 1	2	4[6]	4[6]	7[6] 1	1	1 Ph.M., 1 LL.B.
Minn.	6	24						1	2	2	1[7]	1[3]	2	1	
Mo.	7	18						1		3	1	1[3]	2[3]	1[2]	1 M.S.D.
Neb.	8	22		1				1		1	4		2	$1\frac{1}{6}$	
Dakotas.	9	7	4					1	2		1		2		
Dakotas.	10	10								2	1	2	1		
Dakotas.	11†	14									1	1	3[7]		
Wis.	12	19	7		1			2	2			2		1	
Wis.	13	20			1			3	2	1	1	1	2[4]	2	1 Ph.M.
Total	13	313	45	6	5			15	21 1	17	20	16	46 2	15	11 special.

* 16 without any degrees are graduates of this school.

† 7 are graduates of normal schools.

TABLE XVII—*Concluded*

WESTERN STATES

	School.	Professional Dept.	Training Dept.	Pd. B.	Pd. M.	Pd. D.	M. E.	B. L.	Ph. B.	B. S.	A. B.	S. M.	A. M.	Ph. D.	Special.
III Ariz.	1	7					1			1				1	
	2	20								2	1		3	1	
Cal.	3	26	7					1	1[2]			1	3[7]	2[7][1]	1 B. P. 1 M. L.
Col.	4	24		4	2					2	1	2	4[3]	3	
Mon.	5	9						2			1	1	2	1	
N. M.	6	9								3				1	1 B. Acct.
Wash.	7	13							1		1		2	2	
Ore.	8	17								1	4		1		4 B. S. D.
Ida.	9	10								1	2		2[7]		
Total	9	135	7	4	2		1	3	2	10	10	4	17	11	7 Special.

SOUTHERN STATES

	School.	Professional Dept.	Training Dept.	Pd. B.	Pd. M.	Pd. D.	M. E.	B. L.	Ph. B.	B. S.	A. B.	S. M.	A. M.	Ph. D.	Special.
IV Ark.	1	5									2			1[1]	1 L. I.
Fla.	2	6									1				2 L. I.
Ga.	3	5	3							1	2				
	4	14											4		1 B. E.
Vir.	5	12									3		1	1	
W. Vir.	6	8									2		1		
Total	6	50	3							1	10		6	2	4 Special.
Grand Total	49	875	188	12	8		46	19	24	34	65	29	117	53	34 Special.
								1	2	3			3		

The following table shows the totals in the four groups:

TABLE XVIII.

	No. of Teachers.	Pd B.	Pd. M.	M. E.	B. L.	Ph. B.	B. S.	A. B.	S. M.	A. M.	Ph. D.	Special.
N. Eastern States	377	2	1	45	1	1	6	25	9	48	25	12
W. Central States	313	6	5		15	21	17	20	16	46	15	11
Western States	135	4	2	1	3	2	10	10	4	17	11	7
Southern States	50						1	10		6	2	4
Totals	875	12	8	46	19	24	34	65	29	117	53	34

Let us group these, as with the New York schools, into pedagogical, collegiate, higher, and special degrees.

Pedagogical degrees: Pd. B.; Pd. M.; M. E.[1]

Collegiate   "   B. L.; Ph. B.; B. S.; A. B.

Higher   "   S. M.; A. M.; Ph. D.

TABLE XIX (1).

	No. of teachers.	Pedagogical.	Collegiate.	Higher.	Special.
N. Eastern States	377	48	33	82	12
W. Central States	313	11	73	77	11
Western States	135	7	25	32	7
Southern States	50		11	8	4
Total	875	66	142	199	34

Expressing these in per cent of the number of teachers,

---

[1] The M. E. is the "Master of Elementary Didactics" degree. This was at one time given by the Normal Schools of Pennsylvania, but has now been discontinued.

we have the following: showing, also, the percentage of teachers having no degree at all.

TABLE XIX (2).

	No. of teachers.	Pedagogical.	Collegiate.	Higher.	Special.	No degree.
N. Eastern States..	100	15	9	22	3	51
W. Central States..	100	3	23	24	3	47
Western States....	100	5	19	24	5	47
Southern States...	100		22	16	8	54
	100	8	16	23	4	49

Comparing these figures with those for New York, we have:

	Pedagogical.	Collegiate.	Higher.	Special.	No degrees.
New York.............	2	28	10	3	58
Other States..........	8	16	23	4	49—

The large percentage holding pedagogical degrees in " other states " is due to the early practice in the Pennsylvania schools, already referred to. The lower percentage holding collegiate degrees—16 as compared with 28—is doubtless due to the inaccuracy of the data, in that 23 per cent are assigned to the higher degrees, while many of these are doubtless holders of collegiate degrees as well. If we assume that in " other states " the percentage of instructors having higher degrees without collegiate is that of New York, viz.: 10 per cent, we would then have practically the same percentage of collegiate degrees, viz.: 29. This assumption is probably not far from the truth. Those having special degrees are practically the same. The above figures show that 58 per cent of the New York Normal School teachers have no degrees: while in " other states," there are only 49 per cent. Yet these figures are probably, in reality, practically the same. Seventy per cent of all the pedagogical degrees in " other states " are the M. E., now discarded by the very schools which once gave them. This means, essentially, that 70 per cent of these 8 per cent must be ranked with those having no degree. This leaves only about 2 per cent in " other states " holding pedagogical degrees, and gives 55 per cent having no degrees.

Thus we conclude that the standing of the teachers in the Empire State Normal Schools is practically typical of that throughout the Normal Schools of the country. Or, in other words, the low standard in the New York schools, as pointed out above, is typical of the Normal Schools of the country; and all conclusions reached with reference to the former are substantiated by a study of the larger group.

The holding of degrees—as discussed above—is only one of many standards by which one's preparation for an educational position may be estimated. Too much must not be based on that standard. Too much must not be based on any one standard. One other standard may be here briefly considered. This is that of contributions to educational literature.

This surely must not be considered a very safe standard. There are teachers, and there are writers. Greatness in the former does not necessarily suggest power in the latter. " Dr. Nicholas Murray Butler, in the Educational Review protesting against Dr. Stanley Hall's magnifying research and investigation as a necessary element in a progressive and effectual scholar, says: ' It must be borne in mind that productive scholarship and printing are far from being identical. The highest type of productive scholarship in our day finds its expression through *will* work in institutions, great and small.' " [1] President Butler would doubtless apply this principle to the teacher. The highest type of efficient teaching is in " will work " in the class room, rather than in contributions to the press.

[1] *American Education*, vol. v, p. 79.

On the other hand, there is much in President Hall's emphasis upon the value of research and investigation, as a necessary element in progressive and effectual educational work. This element is a necessary prerequisite to valuable contributions to educational literature. It is just as essential to progressive and efficient teaching. One who is making such progress through some form of research will doubtless make his advancement known through books or educational periodicals. Thus contributions to current educational literature form probably another actual criterion of the interest and progressiveness in educational work on the part of our Normal School instructors.

To this end I have examined all the articles published in 1895, 1900, and 1903, in six of our leading educational periodicals (with one exception, *American Education,* which was not easily accessible for just these dates). As is well known, Normal Schools have laid considerable emphasis upon psychology. It is not, then, out of place to consider here two psychological magazines. Except in the *School Review,* all " Reviews " are included as regular articles. The contributors are divided in four groups: 1. Normal School teachers; 2. Public School teachers, including principals and superintendents; 3. College and University instructors; 4. Others, including business men, public officials, and the writers of unsigned articles.

The figures given in Table XX, page 150 are subject to some criticism, by reason of the indefiniteness of the fourth group. This includes all articles not classed in one of the other three groups. This includes a large number where no signature is given, or where I was unble to locate the author by his name alone. The importance, however, of these figures lies in the relations among the other three columns.

Out of a total of 1438 articles examined, only 78, or about 5 per cent, are contributed by Normal School men: 13 per cent are contributed by teachers in the Public Schools; 48 per cent are contributed by college instructors. We must not place too much dependence on these figures: but they do measure the relatively small amount contributed to educational literature by Normal School instructors. As pointed out above, this is one of many tests of activity in educational problems.

TABLE XX

	Normal School	Public School	College and University	Others	Total
Psychological Review..........1895			73	59	
1900			60	41	
1903			95	9	
Total...........			228	109	337
American Jour. of Psy. 1895			25	14	
1900	2		14	17	
1903			36	2	
Total...........	2		75	33	110
Educational Review...........1895	7	20	72	27	
1900	13	9	55	34	
1903	3	20	54	21	
Total...........	23	49	181	82	335
Education 1895	5	16	23	50	
1900	6	18	15	54	
1903	5	11	11	33	
Total...........	16	45	49	137	247
School Review 1895	3	19	64	23	
1900	3	12	41	20	
1903	2	17	23	14	
Total...........	8	48	128	57	241
Pedagogical Seminary 1895	1		7	18	
1900	1		9	17	
1903	4		11	2	
Total...........	6		27	37	70
American Education 1901–2	4	25	2	7	
1903–4	19	24	2	15	
Total...........	23	49	4	22	148
Grand Total	78	191	692	477	1438

BIBLIOGRAPHY

Special references are made to the following:

American Journal of Instruction, 1830, 1833, 1835, 1841.

Atkinson, F. W. *Professional Preparation of the Secondary Teacher in the United States.*

Barnard, H. *On Normal Schools.*

Boas, ——. *Yale Psychological Studies*, 2: 40.

Brown, E. E. *The Making of Our Middle Schools.*

Butler, N. M. *American Education*, 5: 79.

Common School Journal, 1839, 1840.

Davenport, C. B. *Statistical Methods.*

Gilbert, J. *American Journal of Psychology*, 4: 366.

Gordy, J. P. *Beginning of the Normal Idea in the United States.*

Literary Gazette, 1825.

Meriam, J. L. *American Education*, 1903.

Münsterberg, H. *Atlantic Monthly*, 1903.

North American Review, 1825.

Pearson, K. *Grammar of Science.*

Phillips, J. H. *Chicago School Commission's Report*, 1900.

Potsdam Normal School, *First Quarto-Centennial History of,*

Spearman, C. *American Journal of Psychology*, 1904.

Thorndike, E. L. *Educational Psychology.*
> Lecture Notes, 1903-1904.
> *Mental and Social Measurements.*

United States Review, 1825.

Wissler, C. *Psychological Review Monograph*, 3: no. 6.

REPORTS

Chicago. *Special Commission*, 1900.

Committee of Fifteen.

Illinois. *State Board of Education*, 1900-1902.

Iowa. *State Board of Education*, 1902.

Massachusetts. *State Board of Education*, 1900-1902.

Missouri. *State Superintendent*, 1897.

National Educational Association, 1858-1900.

New York. *State Superintendent,* 1836, 1902.
Ohio. *Commissioner of Common Schools,* 1902.
United States Commissioner of Education, 1897.

CATALOGUES

Albany Academy, 1874.
Albany, Normal College, 1846, 1903, 1904.
Andover Academy, 1848, 1874.
California, University of, 1903.
Chicago University, 1902-1903.
Cincinnati University, 1901-1902.
Cornell University, 1897-1899.
Dartmouth College, 1903-1904.
Illinois Wesleyan University, 1903, 1904.
Los Angeles (Cal.) Normal School, 1901.
Michigan, University of, 1903-1904.
Missouri, University of, 1903-1904.
New Paltz (N. Y.) Normal School, 1902-1903.
Oshkosh (Wis.) Normal School, 1901.
Teachers College, Columbia University, 1904-1905.
Westfield (Mass.) Normal School, 1901.
Wisconsin, University of, 1903-1904.

ERRATA

Page 129. Figure 3 should show 29, instead of 28, holding higher degrees in addition to a college degree. Of these 5, instead of 6, hold pedagogical degrees. The percents in the second part of the figure should be 11 and 2 respectively, instead of 10+ and 2+.